Cost-Benefit Analysis

Issues and Methodologies

A World Bank Publication

Cost-Benefit Analysis

Issues and Methodologies

Anandarup Ray

Published for The World Bank
THE JOHNS HOPKINS UNIVERSITY PRESS
Baltimore and London

First printing May 1984
Second printing July 1986
All rights reserved
Manufactured in the United States of America

The Johns Hopkins University Press
Baltimore, Maryland 21218, U.S.A.

EDITORS   Jane H. Carroll, Christine Houle
PRODUCTION   Christine Houle
BINDING DESIGN   Joyce C. Eisen

Library of Congress Cataloging in Publication Data

Ray, Anandarup.
  Cost-benefit analysis.

  Bibliography: p.
  Includes index.
  1. Cost effectiveness.   I. World Bank.   II. Title.
HD47.4.R39   1984   658.1'554   83–49367
ISBN 0–8018–3068–0
ISBN 0–8018–3069–9 (pbk.)

Contents

Acknowledgments

THIS BOOK was written during my sabbatical leave from the World Bank, from October 1980 to September 1981. I spent the first part of the leave in Oxford as a senior visiting fellow at St. Antony's and the Institute of Economics and Statistics. It would not have been possible to complete the manuscript during that short stay without the excellent facilities that Edward Jackson and Gillian Coates arranged for me at the Institute.

This book evolved out of a series of workshops that I conducted over several years for country and project economists in the World Bank, where the different approaches to cost-benefit analysis continue to be of interest. Many of the participants at the workshops, as well as others who attended various related seminars, indicated that a review of the main controversies in cost-benefit analysis would be useful.

To the extent that this book succeeds in presenting a helpful review, the credit must be shared by all those who created the exciting and pragmatic environment in which I worked. The book reflects the ideas and contributions of many persons, although the points of view expressed are mine. The book does not attempt to represent the Bank's policies and practices in the area of project evaluation. Also, despite the assistance of many friends and colleagues, both in and outside the Bank, I alone am responsible for any shortcomings.

My greatest debt is to Herman van der Tak, with whom I worked for many years in this and related areas. The overview in Chapter 1 is partly adapted from some work we did together. He also helped me with the papers on which Chapters 4 and 6 are partly based. Sudhir Anand's contributions were invaluable in preparing Chapter 3 and the Appendix. The advice and comments I received from Gordon Hughes, James Mirrlees, Pasquale Scandizzo, and Lyn Squire were also particularly helpful. In addition, I would like to acknowledge the help at various stages of Clive Bell, Charles Blitzer, Robin Boadway, Kevin Cleaver, William Cuddihy, Arnold Harberger, Randolph Harris, Bimal Jalan, Deepak Lal, Sanjaya Lall, Per Ljung, Pradeep Mitra, Mohan Munasinghe, Garry Pursell, and Maurice Scott. I am truly grateful to all of them, and to Ann van Aken and Corazon David, who typed successive drafts of the manuscript with care and patience.

Finally, I would like to express my gratitude to Esha and Adi Ray for their encouragement while I was researching and writing this book.

Cost-Benefit Analysis

Issues and Methodologies

CHAPTER 1

Introduction and Overview

COST-BENEFIT ANALYSIS has been a very active field of research and study since at least the early 1960s. Its development has had much to do with the evaluation of public sector investment projects, and it is primarily from this point of view that I approach it in this book. This type of analysis is frequently recommended to public sector agencies as a tool of project evaluation, and some international agencies, such as the World Bank, use it regularly in the course of their operations. The practical importance of cost-benefit analysis is not of course confined to project evaluation. In one form or another, it also bears on such areas as investment planning, commercial policy, and taxation policy—or on "development policy" broadly defined.

There have been numerous important contributions to the theory and practice of cost-benefit analysis. A satisfactory classification of the various contributions is indeed a daunting task. For the purpose of this book a broad dichotomy has been adopted. Economic analysis of projects, in the form in which it has been commonly used over many years, is referred to as the "traditional" approach. Arnold Harberger and Edward Mishan are among its many well-known exponents. In contrast, another approach has emerged which, while very close to the traditional one in many ways, has significant differences. This new method appeals to many because of its apparently closer links to the development literature and to the recent advances in the theory of taxation. Its earliest forms owe much to Stephen Marglin and Amartya Sen. Martin Feldstein was another notable contributor. The operational guidelines of Dasgupta, Marglin, and Sen (1972) consolidated much of the early contributions. Ian Little and James Mirrlees (1968, 1974) developed this approach further in a rather special and highly influential way, as can be seen from the subsequent World Bank publication by Lyn Squire and Herman van der Tak (1975). Much work has since been done, in and outside the World Bank, in experimenting with various methods and techniques. This book consolidates much of the work done in this area in recent years, focusing on those aspects of cost-benefit analysis that continue to be controversial despite many years of debate.

Many of the chapters in this book use material I had prepared, sometimes with my colleagues and friends, for other purposes. Despite my attempts to integrate them smoothly, some disparities in style remain. Also, I have not tried to ensure notational consistency throughout, except when it was critical to do so.

Organization

The discussion begins with an examination of the issue of distribution weights in Chapter 2. Many authors have taken a strong stand against the introduction of differential distribution weights in cost-benefit analysis, and some of them still propagate the view that such analysis can be undertaken without any value judgments. Their opposition is often couched in terms of what economists should or should not do. Attempts are often made, for example, to eliminate the issue by defining economics as a science that does not deal with that issue. These types of argument are examined in Chapter 2 and elsewhere in the book, not only from the theoretical point of view but also from the practical point of view. To put first things first, Chapter 2 discusses individual and social welfare criteria. Since these matters are extensively covered in practically all textbooks on welfare economics and microeconomic theory, only a brief sketch is provided—sufficient, it is hoped, to point out that objectivity in welfare analysis still remains an elusive goal. The role of economic analyses in decisionmaking, especially in the context of project evaluation, is also discussed since some of the polemics on cost-benefit analysis can be traced to differences in assumptions that various authors make in this context.

Chapter 3 continues the discussion of social evaluation issues. It first presents an account of the valuation function now popularly used—especially in the taxation literature. It is hoped that the imponderables in this area are made quite explicit in the process. The traditional valuation function is also discussed, as well as some interesting recent initiatives in devising alternative ways in which distributional concerns can be reflected in policy and project analysis. The valuation functions discussed are indirect and are defined on the price and income space. The price vector, however, is suppressed in that discussion. Some readers may find it interesting to extend the analysis to include the price vector explicitly, thereby linking the discussion formally with the discussions of consumer and producer surpluses elsewhere in the book.

The relative valuation of traded and nontraded goods is discussed in Chapter 4. The contribution of Little and Mirrlees (1974), and its connection to the traditional approach, is considered in some detail. There are many popular fallacies regarding what their technique does and does not do, and whether it is really different from the traditional approach, despite the significant differences in jargon. Since a clear understanding of the various issues in the valuation of traded and nontraded goods is critical to the practice of cost-benefit analysis, a somewhat lengthy presentation has been provided.

Chapter 5 deals with "capital market" issues and reviews the essence of the systems proposed by Dasgupta, Marglin and Sen, Little and Mirrlees, and Squire and van der Tak. The discussion is very selective since a full treatment of discount rate issues would require a separate volume. This chapter begins by distinguishing several kinds of interest rates; it is seen that the use of a single discount rate may logically require the use of differential distribution weights. The relation of market interest rates to the notion of a social discount rate is also shown. The systems of Little and Mirrlees, and of Squire and van der Tak, are then reviewed in detail and compared with the traditional method. Their premium on public income is discussed not only in relation to the marginal value of public expenditures but also in relation to the marginal cost of acquiring public resources. A summary of the basic equations is provided for easy reference.

The choice between the relatively simple traditional approach—perhaps best explained in Harberger (1976, Chap. 7)—and one of the systems referred to above will depend in part on the simplifying assumptions preferred and the issues of interest. If the reader wants to go beyond Harberger, he or she will probably find the subject exciting and insightful, and at the same time quite difficult in practice. Chapters 6 and 7 explore more fully the practical aspects of the new approaches discussed in Chapter 5, including both potential advantages and difficulties.

Chapter 6 illustrates, with numerical examples, the techniques of Little and Mirrlees and Squire and van der Tak. The examples constructed are extremely simple in order to enable the reader to focus on such potentially troublesome issues as the time-dependence of distribution weights and their use when project-induced changes are nonmarginal. Sensitivity analysis is also discussed. These issues cannot be avoided in practice but are not discussed in the literature in any detail.

Chapter 7 summarizes the implications of using variable weights and discusses pricing and cost recovery issues, which are of great interest on their own, apart from being frequently intermingled with project evaluation issues.

Finally, the Appendix provides a concise discussion of shadow wage rates. Many of the available treatments of this topic are taxonomic because the burgeoning empirical literature has not yet been adequately digested from the point of view of shadow pricing. While the taxonomy in the Appendix may be a useful complement to similar treatments, no attempt was made to do justice to the recent research on labor markets, in or outside the World Bank. Such an attempt will clearly be first on the agenda if a revision of this book becomes necessary in the future.

Any discussion of issues in cost-benefit analysis must be placed in its proper context. The nuances of that discussion will depend largely on whether one is talking about practical project evaluation or about more general matters, such as taxation and trade policy. Because of the importance of the context and the highly selective nature of this book, the rest of this chapter attempts to put the discussion in its proper perspective and to provide an overview of the subject for the general reader.

Some General Issues

The principles of economic analysis of projects are exactly the same as the principles of analysis in other branches of applied welfare economics. The distinguishing features of project analysis are twofold: first, project analysis is typically carried out in greater detail and specificity than analyses of sectoral or economywide issues, such as those concerning trade policies and tax structures; and second, it involves a sequential process within the special context of the project cycle. A comprehensive account of the World Bank project cycle is provided in Baum (1978).

The context of the project cycle is important. Economic analysis is not a one-shot affair at the appraisal stage, which immediately precedes the commitment of financial resources to the project. If, as in some cases, it is limited to the appraisal stage, then it can serve only as a final check on the overall soundness of the project proposal. But many of the early decisions made in developing the project may not enter the analysis at the appraisal stage. Questions on the identification of the project and its subsequent formulation in terms of plant size, supporting infrastructure, location, beneficiaries, and so on, may often lose their immediacy and relevance at that stage.

Nor should economic analysis end at the appraisal stage, which may come fairly early or late in the cycle. Substantial work may remain to be done on final design and costing after appraisal. But even after all plans have been finalized, their implementation usually raises new issues. This is especially so in projects with flexible plans, such as rural development projects. Economic analysis should then be an important feature in adapting plans.

Finally, quite apart from the need for ex post evaluation studies to learn from experience, economic analysis continues to be relevant to the operation of project facilities and services throughout their lives. For example, only the broad principles of pricing policies can usually be set at the appraisal stage. The effective implementation of such policies usually requires periodic analysis and revision in the light of evolving circumstances. In short, economic analysis is used to define and resolve issues as one proceeds down the many branches of the decision tree in planning, implementing, and operating a project.

Many believe that the importance of economic analysis in project work can easily be exaggerated. The various activities needed for developing a project, however, should be seen as interdependent, and the question of priorities cannot be meaningfully pursued at the abstract level. The time and effort that should be allocated to economic work at any stage of project development and implementation can be decided only in the light of practical circumstances.

The limitations of data and time and competing priorities often impose serious constraints on the quality and quantity of economic work. Cost-benefit analysis in practice can rarely be conducted in a manner comparable to lengthy research projects. Practical analysts must learn how to use the limited resources at hand most effectively, avoiding excessive detail and spurious precision and employing proxies and shortcuts suitable for the projects they are concerned with. The objective is to do the minimum necessary to resolve issues satisfactorily, rather than to meet puristic standards for their own sake. Practical work is neither for the faint-hearted nor for the perfectionist.

The extent of detail and the form of analysis thus tend to vary considerably. The difficulty of measuring benefits often reduces cost-benefit analysis to cost-minimization exercises in sectors such as health, education, and potable water supply. Even in sectors such as power and telecommunications, economic rates of return often reflect the adequacy or the inadequacy of tariff levels rather than the acceptability of projects. In fact, differences in measurement make the economic rate of return a hazardous tool for allocating investments between sectors.

Difficulty in measuring costs and benefits sometimes makes it impossible to judge a project's merit with much confidence. Alternatively, the variables involved in the analysis, rather than measurement problems, may indicate a "toss-up" situation. Cost-benefit analysis can still be useful in such situations. First, the analysis might indicate ways to improve prospects. For example, if uncertainty about yield increments is the source of the problem in an agricultural project, one can try to discover ways to increase the yield increment to at least the minimum level required for the project to be acceptable. Second, even when risk is not controllable, cost-benefit analysis is still useful for clarifying issues. If in a particular case one cannot say much about a project's merit, this inability in itself should be useful information.

Since cost-benefit analysis, however well done, can be useful only if it is understood and appreciated by nonspecialist decisionmakers, presentation is extremely important. Methodological contributions have recognized this importance. Thus, one method would summarize a project's merit by the foreign exchange earned or saved for each unit of domestic resource costs incurred, while another would measure the net present value (NPV) of the project in a way that makes it equivalent to a grant of fungible foreign exchange from abroad of the same amount. Still others define the NPV measure in terms of changes in domestic income. All these methods are equivalent if the same assumptions and data are used in the analysis.

Whichever presentation is used, a common complaint against cost-benefit analysis is that it collapses a large and intricate story into a single number, such as the economic rate of return (ERR), or the NPV. There is much to this criticism, even though the use of such a summary indicator is simply another way of saying "yes" or "no," which analysts and advisers must ultimately do. Nonetheless, decisionmakers who base their judgments solely on a reported rate of return may well deceive themselves. The rate of return or the NPV is a *relative* statement of a project's merit, not an absolute one. Such measures may sometimes be quite sensitive to the precise way in which the alternatives compared have been defined. Decisionmakers should also understand the nature of the information used, the degree of confidence that can be placed on it, and the basic approach used in the evaluation of costs and benefits in the first place.

The remedy to this problem of presentation is not the production of a multiplicity of indicators. Even the presentation of separate tables on such special features of a project as its effect on the balance of payments and employment may mislead, rather than enlighten, by placing more emphasis on considerations already weighted and incorporated in the economic analysis. There are no general rules in this area since the best practices can be defined only for specific institutional contexts.

It is also sometimes suggested that cost-benefit analysis is not useful unless it is applied systematically across all public sector projects. The domain of cost-benefit analysis is certainly quite restricted in practice. Few developing countries use such analysis widely on a systematic basis. Even if they wished to do so, they would encounter the inherent difficulties in using cost-benefit analysis fully in some sectors, as mentioned earlier. Cost-benefit analysis is not, however, an all-or-nothing proposition. Just as one can evaluate a proposed change in, say, a trade duty, taking the trade regime as a whole as given, one can also evaluate a project, taking the decisions rules for other projects as given.[1] There is no reason to doubt the usefulness of even infrequent applications.

Another complaint against cost-benefit analysis is that it tends to give too much importance to shadow pricing, that is, to the adjustments of financial inflows and outflows to transform them into economic terms. As discussed earlier, the basic options to be analyzed must first be decided before the relevant items of costs and benefits can be identified. This identification and the initial measurement of costs and benefits can often be difficult. In particular, the quality of project economic work tends to depend heavily on how much emphasis is given to the market effects of a project intervention. How will additional power sales affect the usually distorted markets for related products? How will the labor market respond to an irrigation scheme? These and other such questions are often hard to resolve satisfactorily in practice. But unless these problems are handled well, cost-benefit analysis might degenerate into a mechanical routine.

1. The shadow pricing parameters used in cost-benefit analysis may, of course, depend on how widely such analysis is used, but this is a different issue.

Valuation problems are, however, also important. Many popular fallacies tend to nullify the sound and painstaking work that often precedes the application of shadow pricing: "the shadow exchange rate equals the official rate when the balance of payments is healthy," "unemployment of labor means that the shadow wage rate is less than the market rate," and so on. Moreover, most of the shadow prices needed for project evaluation can be properly estimated only by project economists. There are only a few national parameters that the project analyst can take as given.

Nonetheless, it has to be recognized that recommendations on cost-benefit methods to agencies in developing countries should take account of not only the practical problems of analysis in the pertinent sectors but also the institutional capability for project cycle management in general and for cost-benefit analysis in particular. Often the relevant question is whether the recommended method would make project decisions more frequently correct than they otherwise would be, not whether it would make them as frequently correct as ideally possible.

Basic Approaches

Economic benefits and costs of a project can be defined only by the effect of the project on some fundamental objectives of the economy. Given the choice of a fundamental objective, and the precise manner in which it is defined, one obtains a measuring rod, or a common yardstick, to assess the various effects of a project. There is no analytic distinction between benefits and costs. Costs are simply the benefits forgone by not using the project resources in other ways. By measuring both benefits and costs with the same yardstick, one can indicate in project analysis the net impact on the chosen objective. If the net impact is positive, or at least not negative, the indication is that the project resources cannot be used in better ways from the point of view of that objective.[2]

The mainstream, or the traditional, approach emanates, like most applied welfare economics in other areas, from the so-called new welfare economics of the 1940s.[3] The traditional approach is so widely and routinely used that many project analysts are not even aware of its foundations. To many, project analysis appears divorced from fundamental country objectives.

2. This and the following sections are partially based on an internal World Bank paper prepared by the author with Herman van der Tak. See also Ray and van der Tak (1979) for a complementary discussion.

3. This is variously referred to as the "social surplus," or the "economic," or the "efficiency" approach. For excellent discussions of this approach in the context of cost-benefit analysis, see Harberger (1974, 1977), Hirschleifer, DeHaven, and Milliman (1960), Marglin (1962), and Mishan (1975, 1981).

Perhaps the best way to bring out the implications of this approach is to postulate that the country's objective is to maximize the present value of the stream of consumption changes that the use of its resources in any form, such as a project, will lead to. Two issues immediately arise. First, How should consumption changes at any point in time be measured? and second, How should present and future changes be compared?

The first issue is solved in the traditional approach by simply summing all consumption changes, regardless of the characteristics of the groups to which they accrue. Thus, the postulate refers to aggregate equally weighted consumption. Regarding the second issue, the traditional approach assumes that if the private capital market in a developing country were perfect and if there were no taxes or subsidies at the margin on profits and incomes, the market interest rate would be the appropriate rate for discounting future costs and benefits. If the ERR on investments, measured in terms of aggregate consumption, equals that interest rate, the balance between investment and consumption at any point in time would be correct; that is, the economy would be on its optimal growth path.

If the economy were on its optimal growth path, then the objective function can be restated in terms of the maximization of the sum of aggregate consumption (C) and investment (I), that is, national income, at any point in time. Thus, the maximand is simply $C + I$, given that changes in C are equally as valuable as changes in I. Those who use the traditional approach usually talk, not about consumption effects, but about income effects. There is no difference so long as investment is equally as valuable as present consumption at the margin.

Both ways of stating the objective function, however, cannot be strictly equivalent if there are distortions in the capital market. In that case, one must allow for the possibility that the marginal economic returns to investments will exceed the market interest rate. If they do, investments must be more valuable at the margin than present consumption. One would not, then, measure a project's effects as $\Delta C + \Delta I$, but as $\Delta C + \lambda \Delta I$, where λ is the appropriate weight on investments. Nonetheless, the basic point remains: if the economy is not on its optimal growth path, it must be because of distortions in the capital market. Tinkering at the margin with taxes and subsidies may be all that is required to attain optimal growth.

A developing country may, of course, agree with this point of view. But it is not exactly a compelling point of view, especially for the very poor and backward countries where optimal growth, defined in this way, may mean a perpetual commitment to a dismal standard of living. Moreover, a 2 percent rate of growth with an even distribution of benefits is hardly the same as a 2 percent rate of growth with a highly uneven distribution. Tradeoffs between growth and distribution pose important policy choices that cannot be dismissed by putting forward "trickle down" or similar theories of the development process. Whether benefits trickle down or not is an empirical issue that is far from settled. But even if they do, the normative issue of whether the trickle is large enough cannot be avoided.[4]

At any rate, much of the work on growth and development has rejected the social valuation implicit in the traditional approach and has led to the development of a new approach that is quite open-ended in its social valuation. This new approach does not compel one to reject the traditional view, but allows the use of different judgments when considered relevant.[5] Decisionmakers can use it as a flexible tool—for example, to place much greater weight on investments than implied by the traditional approach or to incorporate the objective of redressing poverty and economic inequality.

This new approach has been called "social" to distinguish it from the traditional, or so-called efficiency, approach. The choice of these terms is unfortunate, since "efficiency" analysis also includes social valuation. Efficiency should refer to means, not ends. In the folklore of project work, the term "social" symbolizes loose thinking, and the term "efficiency" is nothing short of being a rallying cry. What decisionmaker would dare argue against efficiency, especially when the end is left unspecified?

If different fundamental objectives are chosen, the valuation of benefits and costs will also differ. The shadow prices used in the new approach are often called social prices to distinguish them from the shadow prices used in the traditional approach, which are correspondingly called efficiency prices. To illustrate, the efficiency shadow wage rate will be the marginal product of labor in certain cases; the social shadow wage rate may differ, however. If the employment of an additional unit of labor in the project would increase labor income, then the social shadow wage rate would reflect, in addition to the effect on output, both the benefit of that increased income in redressing poverty and the cost of any reduced savings and reinvestment.

While the flexibility of the new approach may be welcome, many feel that opening up social valuation issues is not unlike opening Pandora's box. Certainly, no one has established a definitive way of deciding which type of social valuation is most appropriate. Most people would perhaps agree that the traditional view is inappropriate for many developing countries, and for some developed countries as well. But even if so, it is far from easy to decide exactly how a different social valuation scheme should be formulated.

A question frequently asked in this context is: Granted that value judgments must be made, whose judgments are to be used? The answer depends on the person or persons for whom the analysis is being conducted. For example, an economist might independently carry out a cost-benefit study for debates on a project or simply as an academic exercise. In that

---

4. See Chenery (1974) for an extensive discussion of such issues in a wider policy context.

5. See, for example, Dasgupta, Marglin, and Sen (1972), Little and Mirrlees (1974), and Squire and van der Tak (1975).

case, the economist should obviously use the judgments that appeal most to him. Alternatively, cost-benefit analysis might be carried out to assist an international or bilateral—that is, "foreign"—agency or a national public sector agency.

A foreign agency does not usually undertake projects, it finances them. The decision to finance a project, its rationale, and the processes by which it is reached are the responsibility of the foreign agency, not that of the borrower. If the financing decision is based on cost-benefit analysis, the value judgments used are also the responsibility of that agency. Of course, the agency may, if it chooses, try to ensure that such judgments are consistent with the preferences of the government in the country concerned, as far as such preferences can be determined.

Agencies within the public sector in the country should follow the preferences of the top-level unit, whether an interministerial investment board or a planning commission, which screens project proposals and advises the ultimate decisionmakers. Centralized direction is presumed because without it the value of cost-benefit analysis becomes indeterminate. Without central direction on the methods to be used, for example, an irrigation agency and a highway agency may use different shadow wage rates for the same labor in the same area; alternatively, they may use different discount rates. But if lower-level agencies perceive a consistent demand for cost-benefit analysis from the top—the critical requirement—then the trial-and-error process will lead to norms and conventions which directly or indirectly reflect how top-level units prefer to receive information. It is quite possible, of course, that cost-benefit analysis will be demanded for projects in only some sectors, or only for projects costing sizable amounts, or only for projects financed from abroad. But restricted applications of cost-benefit analysis need not make it useless, although inconsistent applications will certainly do so.

Valuation of Costs and Benefits

The traditional approach, as noted earlier, focuses on changes in total consumption a project is expected to produce over time. These changes can be expressed either in domestic values or in border values; the choice of the unit of account is immaterial to the analysis as long as it does not affect the relative prices of the various inputs and outputs.[6]

It has been customary in traditional practice to express costs and benefits in domestic prices, converting the foreign values of traded inputs and

6. The border value of a traded commodity is its CIF (cost, insurance, and freight) or FOB (free on board) price expressed in units of domestic currency at the official exchange rate. The domestic values of nontraded commodities are converted to border values by techniques discussed in the next section.

outputs to domestic values by using a shadow exchange rate. This shadow exchange rate is intended to adjust the relative prices of traded and nontraded goods, which are usually distorted by various trade interventions, such as import and export duties and quantitative restrictions, as well as by other measures. Accounting in terms of border values, however, has become very common. This involves the reverse process of converting domestic values of nontraded inputs and outputs to border values by using conversion factors, which remove the distortions in their relative prices.

Costs and benefits can also be expressed in border values in the new approach. But the common yardstick is different because of differences in the basic policy objectives underlying the analysis. First, consumption gains and losses to different income groups may be weighted differently, with unit weight assigned to (small) consumption changes at a particular level of consumption, such as the national average level. Second, since investment may also be valued differently from consumption, all values must be measured either in terms of consumption or in terms of investment (or, more broadly, nonconsumption expenditures). In the Little–Mirrlees version of the new approach, which has gained wide currency, investment is chosen as the common yardstick, or numeraire. Often, further distinctions are made between different kinds of expenditures other than consumption, and in such cases the numeraire is conventionally chosen to be discretionary public income valued in border prices, that is, "uncommitted foreign exchange" in the hands of the government.

Valuation of foreign and domestic goods

The convention of expressing all costs and benefits in border values, or "foreign exchange," was introduced by Little and Mirrlees. This convention gives their technique much of its distinctive jargon and flavor. Many have found it difficult to translate their messages into traditional terms, as is evident from the polemical literature on the subject.

Jargon apart, the key point in Little–Mirrlees is that the shadow exchange rate should not be uniquely defined: there should be, in principle, as many shadow exchange rates as nontraded goods in the economy. This has led to much controversy, partly because the concept of the shadow exchange rate, so commonly used in traditional practice, has itself been defined in conflicting ways.

The basic message is quite simple and can be summarized as follows: some inputs and outputs of the project affect, directly or indirectly, the level of imports; other inputs and outputs affect, again directly or indirectly, the level of exports. The value to the economy of such traded goods is measured by border prices, namely CIF or FOB prices, suitably adjusted for internal transport and other costs. If, however, import prices rise or export prices fall on account of the project, the value to the economy of additional imports or exports is not measured by the old or the new border price but by the marginal import or export revenue, which are better approximations to that value.

The value of nontraded goods is measured in the first instance by domestic market prices prior to necessary adjustments. If the use of a nontraded input by the project affects only the amount of use by others, the shadow price of the input should be derived from its marginal value (demand price). However, cases in which the input supply is completely fixed rarely occur. Often, the project affects only the production of the input; the shadow price of the input should then be derived from its marginal cost (supply price). If the project affects both production of the input and its available supply to others, the shadow price of the input is derived from a weighted average of the demand and supply prices. If a project produces a nontraded good, its value is also derived from its domestic market price. Incremental consumer surplus because of any project-induced changes in that price should also be taken into account.

If accounting is done in terms of border values, the domestic values of nontraded inputs and outputs must be converted to border values. The appropriate conversion factors depend on whether supply or demand prices, or some average of the two, are relevant. When the supply price of a nontraded good is relevant, the appropriate conversion factor represents a revaluation of the domestic cost of production in terms of border prices: it is the ratio of the cost in border prices to the cost in domestic prices. Such conversion factors for adjusting supply prices differ among nontraded goods so that, in principle, there is not one general conversion factor for all nontraded goods but a large set of such factors.

When the project increases the prices for nontraded inputs, or produces nontraded outputs, the domestic demand prices become relevant. The conversion factor that adjusts the demand price for a commodity is a weighted average of the conversion factors of the various goods and services that substitute for, or complement, that commodity. As in the case of conversion factors for supply prices, there is, in principle, a separate conversion factor for the demand price of each nontraded good.

In practice, of course, it is not feasible to differentiate conversion factors for all nontraded commodities. Shortcuts that provide reasonable approximations are needed. In essence, all the shortcuts involve some degree of averaging for a group of nontraded items. For example, separate conversion factors might be estimated for broad groups of items such as construction, transport, or consumption. The consumption conversion factor may be further differentiated by income groups or by rural and urban areas. Nonetheless, the use of such averages permits greater accuracy than the use of a single "standard" conversion factor for all nontraded items, which is inversely proportional to the common definition of the shadow exchange rate.[7]

The standard conversion factor or, equivalently, the economywide shadow exchange rate, is usually calculated as a summary indicator of trade distortions expected to be in force in the future. This is not a question of equilibrium in the balance of payments, or of scarcity of foreign exchange faced by developing countries. Even if there is no apparent balance of payments problem, or even if the actual exchange rate is allowed to adjust freely, the standard conversion factor may be less than unity or, equivalently, the shadow exchange rate may be greater than the actual exchange rate because of import duties, export subsidies, and quantitative trade restrictions. The shadow exchange rate will also equal the actual rate; that is, the standard conversion factor will also be unity, if by pure chance all the various distortions precisely offset each other. Such possibilities emphasize the need for using disaggregative conversion factors whenever feasible.

Conversion factors are usually estimated on the assumption that trade and taxation policies and the real exchange rate will on the whole remain unchanged. But this assumption may be inappropriate if, for instance, shadow prices are being estimated when a country has initiated a stabilization policy that will take effect in a few years. This topic is discussed in Chapter 6.

The discount rate and distribution weights

The new approach mainly concerns differential weighting of gains and losses to different individuals, both at a point in time and over time. The conceptual issues are discussed in Chapters 2, 3, and 5. Chapters 6 and 7 focus instead on practical issues, illustrating the mechanics and scope of the new approach. Some general aspects of this discussion are summarized below.

The question of which discount rate is appropriate for cost-benefit analysis has long been a favorite topic among economists. In a sense this issue is trivial. Whichever approach one adopts, the basic discount rate must be the "consumption rate of interest" which, by definition, indicates the rate at which the value of consumption falls over time. But whose consumption and whose valuation?

In traditional analysis, it is the valuation reflected in the market interest rate that is used for reference. If all individuals participate in the capital market and if there are no distortions in that market, that interest rate will

---

7. The standard conversion factor equals the ratio of the official exchange rate to the shadow exchange rate as defined here.

indeed reflect a common valuation within the present generation. This common consumption rate of interest may also equal the private return to investment at the margin. In practice, the equality of these interest rates may not of course be attained. But if it were attained, and if, in addition, this interest rate equaled the marginal economic returns to investment, this approach would imply, as noted earlier, that additional savings and investment to promote growth are as valuable as additional current consumption.

A developing country may, however, set the consumption rate of interest exogenously, either because the market does not reveal a common rate (if a proper market exists in the first place) or because it views the market rate as being too low or too high. Economic theory suggests that the market interest rate will indicate the discount rate appropriate for intergenerational comparisons only under very unrealistic assumptions. If the discount rate is set differently from the marginal economic returns to investment, then an investment premium, or discount, should be introduced in the analysis. The shadow interest rate will then depend on whether consumption or investment is the chosen numeraire. If costs and benefits are expressed in terms of investments, the shadow interest rate will equal the rate at which the value of investment falls over time—the "accounting rate of interest." This accounting rate of interest is the cut-off rate for social analysis of projects, that is, the social rate of return on investments at the margin, when investment is the chosen numeraire. This is also the "opportunity cost of capital," or the "marginal productivity of capital," in terms of the objective function used in that framework.

If investment is the chosen numeraire, then the value of project-induced consumption changes in any year must be reduced by the investment premium. The usual procedure is first to measure net project benefits in efficiency prices and in border values and then to subtract from this total an amount equal to the net cost of any additional consumption due to the project. This net cost will be higher, the higher the investment premium. The annual net benefits thus calculated should then be discounted at the accounting rate of interest. The NPV calculated in this way would then incorporate a correction for the intertemporal imbalance between investment and consumption.

Although it may not always be possible to identify the savings effects of a project, and although the appropriate size of the investment premium can be only roughly estimated, consistent analysis requires that the same premium be used in evaluating the reinvestments generated by different projects in a country. Similarly, if concerns with income inequality or poverty alleviation are relevant to project decisions in a country, they should be reflected in a consistent manner. Uncertainty as to which particular values of distribution or poverty weights are most appropriate is bound to exist. However, if such weights are not made explicit, widely different values are likely to be used implicitly in project decisions. The difficulties in choosing the most appropriate definition of poverty or in fixing the "right" weights do not negate the need for consistency.

The analysis with an investment premium penalizes all increases in consumption regardless of the income status of the recipients. But consumption gains may be valued more highly if the recipients are poor. If, for example, the recipients are close to or below the absolute poverty line, additional consumption gains may in fact be regarded as a net social benefit rather than a net cost. The break-even line above which consumption gains represent a net social cost, and below which a net social gain, is called the "critical consumption level." This critical consumption level is usually judged to lie below the income level at which income taxes first become payable.

In specifying the weights to be assigned to consumption gains accruing to different income levels, a distinction between only a few levels may suffice. The weights may be made consistently progressive—the lower the income level, the greater the weight, with a weight of unity being given to the national per capita level. Alternatively, equal weights may be assigned to all income groups except the lowest. The traditional practice of assigning equal weights to all income levels is clearly a special case.

Consumption changes may arise if some of the suppliers of inputs to the project, including labor, are paid more by the project than they would be elsewhere. Such changes will also occur if the prices of the outputs with the project are lower than they would be without the project, that is, if there are changes in consumer surplus. Distribution or poverty weights can be applied only if the consumption changes resulting from the project and the income groups of the beneficiaries to which they accrue can be reasonably determined, which is a difficult task in many cases.

Shadow wage rates

Two sources of controversy exist regarding the shadow pricing of labor. First, the concept differs in the traditional and the new approaches, since the latter emphasizes the consumption cost of employment while the former does not. But this controversy has really nothing to do with actual labor; it simply reflects the controversies regarding the discount rate and distribution weights discussed above. Second, there are different views of labor markets, and of rural-urban migration in particular. Since empirical research on labor markets and migration in developing countries has only recently begun on a serious scale, generalizations would be quite inappropriate at this stage. Shadow pricing of labor is therefore discussed only cursorily in the Appendix.

Investment Criteria

Much of the literature on cost-benefit analysis has focused on the measures by which the economic criterion for project investments should be defined—the net present value (NPV), the economic rate of return (ERR), the cost-benefit ratio, the pay-back period, the first-year rule for timing projects, and so on. Since this literature is not reviewed elsewhere in the book, the basic NPV rule in economic analysis is briefly described here. All special forms of the investment criterion should be tested against this rule to determine their validity (see Harberger, 1976, Chap. 2 for a helpful discussion).

The basic rule applies equally to both the traditional and the new approaches. The magnitudes (and signs) of NPV may differ, but its role in the criterion does not. But since a project considered acceptable in the traditional approach may not appear so in the new, and vice versa, many believe that a compromise between the two approaches may be devised through the use of a "hybrid" criterion (Harberger, 1978). This issue, discussed in Chapter 2, is also introduced below.

The basic rule

Since the maximand in economic analysis is simply the NPV of consumption changes (however weighted) over time, the basic criterion for the acceptability of a project is the present value of its net benefits—the benefits and costs being defined in incremental terms as compared with the situation without the project. It is convenient to state this criterion in two parts.

First, the present value of the net benefits of the project must not be negative. Second, the NPV of the project must be higher than, or at least as high as, the NPV of mutually exclusive project alternatives. There are usually many projects, or project options, which by their nature are mutually exclusive: if one is chosen, the other cannot be undertaken. This applies to different designs, or sizes, or time phases of what is essentially the same project. It also applies, perhaps less obviously, to such cases as plants in alternative locations that serve the same limited market, the development of surface irrigation to the exclusion of tubewell irrigation, and river development upstream instead of downstream. It should not be assumed too easily that such mutually exclusive options do not exist. The need to compare mutually exclusive options is one of the principal reasons for applying economic analysis from the early stages of the project cycle.

Sometimes the measurement of the relevant costs and benefits may require the careful examination of the best alternative options. An agricultural project, for example, may use undeveloped land for which there is no readily apparent market. The opportunity cost of such land may be mistaken to be zero, or very low, unless its best alternative use is identified. Thus, the project may show a high NPV simply because the alternative uses of the land (for growing other crops, for example) have not been considered. Another example is projects that use natural gas, such as some fertilizer projects. The marginal cost of using the gas may appear to be negligibly low unless alternative projects, such as liquefaction of gas for export, are considered. Although, in principle, all meaningful project options should be considered, in practice only a few can usually be examined. A high NPV may therefore reflect an inadequate search for alternative projects rather than a potentially valuable project.

The most popular measure for defining the economic criterion is, however, the internal ERR, that is, the rate of discount that results in a zero NPV for the project. If this rate equals or exceeds the relevant shadow interest rate, then the NPV will not be negative and will thus satisfy the first part of the criterion described above. But the rate of return concept should be avoided in comparing mutually exclusive project alternatives. In such comparisons, the project with the highest rate of return is not necessarily the one with the highest NPV and is therefore not necessarily the best project. While a variant of the rate of return technique can be used to indicate the correct choice in such cases, it is usually cumbersome and prone to error. The rate of return technique is therefore not fully satisfactory. It is nonetheless widely understood and will, no doubt, continue to be used widely, if only for the purpose of presenting the results of analysis.

Many projects combine components dealing with different sectors and activities. For example, a project may combine irrigation with power generation and potable water supply, or it may combine farming with rural roads and the formation and improvement of villages. When the various components are significantly interrelated, neither costs nor benefits can be meaningfully allocated to individual components in the economic analysis. Separate ERRs for the various components cannot be accurately calculated in such cases on the basis of arbitrary prorating of costs and benefits. The appropriate procedure is to calculate the NPV of the entire package, and then to test whether it can be increased by redesigning the project to delete one or more of the components in the package. (See van der Tak, 1966, for a discussion of these issues in the context of power projects.)

The economic analysis of projects is necessarily based on uncertain future events and inaccurate data, and therefore inevitably involves probability judgments, whether made explicit or not. The basic elements in the cost and benefit streams, such as input and output prices and quantities or the economywide shadow pricing parameters, are seldom reasonably represented by single values. It is desirable, therefore, that cost-benefit analyses consider the range of possible variations in the values of the basic elements, and present clearly the extent of the uncertainties attaching to the outcome.

A simple method of doing so is to determine how sensitive the NPV is to changes in the variables or, alternatively, how much a variable must change for the NPV to be reduced to zero. The value of a variable at which the NPV becomes zero is its "switching" or "cross-over" value. Switching-value tests are often particularly helpful in providing a better understanding of the critical elements on which the outcome of the project depends. They may focus attention on the variables for which a further effort should be made to firm up the estimates and narrow down the range of uncertainty. They may also aid the management of the project by indicating critical areas that require close supervision to ensure the expected favorable return to the economy.

Sensitivity analysis, however, does not show the combined net effect of changes in all variables or the likelihood of various changes occurring together. Risk analysis, or probability analysis, can throw light on these question by specifying, as well as possible, probabilities for the several values that may be attained by each variable in the project analysis, as well as how changes in one variable are correlated with changes in the others. The resulting probability distribution of the NPV (or rate of return) gives the decisionmaker a better picture of the degree of risk involved in the project than the one given by a single value calculation. On the basis of such a distribution, judgments can be made as to the existence of, for instance, an X percent chance that the project will result in a negative NPV.

Risk analysis provides a better basis for judging the relative merits of alternative projects—but it does nothing to diminish the risks themselves. Some risks, of course, can be reduced by further investigation of the causes, as in the case of technical problems of production or arrangements for marketing. Whether this is worthwhile depends on the cost of the investigation, the expected reduction in risk, and the value attached thereto. Risk may also be reduced by making the design of the project flexible enough to leave future options open and adjust to unexpected changes in circumstances. Such flexible design is likely to impose additional costs that may or may not be justified.

"Hybrid" criteria

It is often suggested that one should invent mixed criteria to "resolve" the conflicts between the traditional and the new approaches. The most common suggestion is that the NPV tests should be satisfied by both approaches. This, however, is likely to be an impossible task in many cases, since a project has to pass many NPV tests, not one. Even if both types of NPV are nonnegative compared with the "without-project" alternative, the earlier NPV comparisons among mutually exclusive options are likely to lead to conflicts. If conflicts never arose, then either approach would suffice and separate tests would be unnecessary.

Alternatively, one might use the traditional approach for the final test and the new approach for the earlier tests, or the converse. (According to Harberger, 1978, the former alternative would give priority to the traditional approach and the converse, to the new.) Such hybrid criteria are, however, logically inconsistent, and they will not help the decisionmakers control tradeoffs between efficiency and other considerations; that is, they will not help ensure that social objectives are being met at minimum efficiency costs. It can be shown very easily that the effective control of such tradeoffs requires consistent use of the new approach. This is discussed in the appendix to Chapter 2.

CHAPTER 2

The Issue of Distribution Weights

THE USE OF VARIABLE WEIGHTS on gains and losses to different income groups has been the most controversial issue in cost-benefit analysis in recent years. Many considerations have been raised in discussions of this issue, ranging from practical and procedural questions to moral values and political processes.

It is often suggested that the use of distribution weights in economic analysis introduces a political and arbitrary judgment about basic values from which such analysis should be kept free. Thus, "the best thing that economists can do may well be simply to inform their clientele (be it a bureau, a legislature, an interest group, or the public at large) of the strictly economic (i.e., efficiency) costs and benefits expected to result from a particular measure, and to leave it in their hands to decide whether these economic benefits outweigh what may be adjudged non-economic costs, or (vice versa) whether the non-economic benefits are large enough to outweigh the net costs of the measure as estimated by the economist. At the very least, the above position is a perfectly respectable one for economists to take, as indeed a great many do."[1]

This position, which is indeed shared by a great many, rests on two propositions: (1) it is possible to conduct economic analysis strictly in "efficiency" terms, without bringing in distributional weights, and (2) the decisionmaking process is such that the most helpful contribution the economist can make is to calculate only the efficiency net benefits of a project or a policy, leaving it to the decisionmakers to trade off those benefits against noneconomic objectives. These two propositions are examined in this chapter.

Welfare Criteria

The mainstream or traditional criterion of cost-benefit analysis measures the net benefits of a project as its net effect, over time, on the path of total real consumption (aggregated over individuals) in the economy. Since consumption and savings (private and public) are equally valued in the

1. Harberger (1978b). For a more complete statement along these lines, see Harberger (1982).

traditional analysis, the criterion can be restated in terms of real income, rather than consumption. The net effects on real income are measured as the equally weighted sum of consumer and producer surpluses and losses.[2]

Two issues arise in this process: the valuation of the gains and losses accruing to an individual, and their aggregation across individuals, both at a point in time and over succeeding generations. The controversy over distribution weights concerns aggregation, but the valuation of gains to an individual is also sometimes thought to be important in this context and is discussed first below.

Valuation of gains to an individual

If a project leads to a lower price for its output, the welfare gain to individual consumers is commonly defined as the "compensating variation" (CV), that is, the maximum amount of money the consumer can pay and still be no worse off compared with the situation that would prevail without the price change. For noninferior goods, the CV exceeds the area under the Marshallian demand curve. The Marshallian measure in turn exceeds the "equivalent variation" (EV), defined as the amount of money needed to compensate the individual consumer if the price change does not take place. The CV and EV may be defined precisely as follows: Let $e(p^1/p^0, y^0)$ be the expenditure function, indicating the least income required by a consumer facing a new price, p^1, to attain the same utility level as under the parameters p^0, y^0 (the initial price and income, respectively). Then $\text{CV} \equiv e(p^0/p^0, y^0) - e(p^1/p^0, y^0)$, and $\text{EV} \equiv e(p^1/p^1, y^0) - e(p^0/p^1, y^0)$. If M is the Marshallian measure, then $\text{CV} \geq M \geq \text{EV}$ for noninferior goods, and $\text{CV} \leq M \leq \text{EV}$ for an inferior good. $\text{CV} = M = \text{EV}$ when the good in question has zero income elasticity.

The accuracy with which surpluses can be measured has long been a subject of controversy. Willig (1976) provides a method for estimating CV and EV from data that are not always difficult to obtain: the Marshallian measure, the prechange income, and the upper and lower bounds for the income elasticity of demand. He also shows that in many cases the errors from using the Marshallian measure will tend to be less than 2 percent. Hausman (1981), however, shows that if a market demand function is estimated in the conventional way, one can derive the compensated function, by using duality theory, to obtain precise measures of CV and EV — the Willig approximation is not necessary. Moreover, the Willig approximation can easily be very inaccurate for the "deadweight" part of the welfare change (that is, the triangle measure) in which one is usually interested.

2. For example, see Harberger (1974), Marglin (1962), and Mishan (1975, 1981).

Measurement of surpluses, especially in the context of project evaluation, is usually quite difficult. Satisfactory econometric estimates of demand functions are infrequently available. Moreover, measuring the expected price change itself is often difficult, especially in the presence of quantity rationing, which is common in many developing countries, for example, in the public utility sector. In addition, output price changes induced by projects are sometimes large. Simple linear approximations might not be satisfactory in such cases.

The difficulties are compounded when several prices are expected to change simultaneously in response to the change in the price of a product relevant to the project. The assumption in adding up surpluses must then be either that the income effects generated by the price changes are small or that the income elasticities of the goods in question are equal. If the assumption regarding income elasticities holds, the surplus measures will be "path-independent." Path independence is implicitly assumed in many expositions of these concepts, for example, Harberger (1974) and van der Tak and Ray (1971). Ng (1979) provides a simple proof of this assumption concerning income elasticities.

These problems of measuring surpluses with reasonable accuracy limit the reliability of all methods of cost-benefit analysis and therefore do not bear on which method to use. The advantage of the traditional method arises essentially from the simpler aggregation procedure. In practice, one has to measure the gains and losses to groups, which may be broad and heterogeneous. If all individuals are treated equally, much of the gains and losses of individual producers and consumers resulting from a project can be canceled out. One can thus avoid some of the measurement problems more readily with the traditional approach.[3] By contrast, differential treatment may require bold assumptions about the composition of each group and the distribution of project costs and benefits. Thus the scope of any approach that uses differential weights must be more restricted.

Aggregate welfare tests

The least controversial welfare criterion in economics is the Pareto criterion, which simply says that a project must be desirable if nobody loses and at least one person gains.[4] It is also useless since a project that does not hurt anyone has not been discovered yet. A meaningful criterion must be able to resolve conflicts.

3. This will become apparent in the subsequent discussion of the mechanics of using unequal distribution weights in Chapter 6. Much of the discussion in Harberger (1978a) is intended to highlight the additional difficulties, and quite correctly so.
4. The limitations of the Pareto criterion are discussed in Sen (1979).

The famous criterion of Kaldor tries to overcome the problem by suggesting that a project should be regarded as a *potential* improvement if the gainers can, in principle, compensate the losers even though, in practice, they would not do so. In other words, a project is acceptable if the algebraic sum of individual compensating variations is not negative (that is, $\sum \mathrm{CV} \geq 0$). The CV, rather than the EV, is the natural surplus concept to use in this context.

The traditional approach in cost-benefit analysis is often interpreted in the sense of Kaldorian compensation tests.[5] For the present purpose, it is not necessary to discuss the deficiencies of the Kaldor criterion even on its own terms (it can lead to inconsistent rankings) or of the alternatives proposed subsequently by Hicks, Scitovsky, and Little.[6] It is well known that the logical problems with the Kaldor test can be overcome by assuming that all individuals possess linear and identical Engel curves,[7] an assumption that cannot be expected to hold generally in practice.

The fundamental problem with this approach is a very simple one. Since it refers to *potential* welfare rather than to *actual* welfare, the Kaldor criterion is not by itself a welfare criterion. Investment decisions are made on the basis of changes expected in actual welfare, not on changes in potential welfare. Unless decisionmakers can ensure that all project benefits are redistributed at no cost (in which case the Kaldor criterion is redundant), the link between potential welfare in the sense of $\sum \mathrm{CV} \geq 0$ and actual welfare is not straightforward.[8] It is not possible to separate "equity" and "efficiency" issues.[9]

5. See, for example, Mishan (1975).

6. See Layard and Walters (1978) and Sen (1963, 1970).

7. Identical and quasi-homothetic preferences will also suffice if all consumers have sufficiently high incomes to consume at least some of each good affected by a project. It might be noted that the logical inconsistency possible with the Kaldor test arises from the need to use intermediate points to compare points on different but intersecting utility possibility curves. However, such points can be compared directly if welfare weights are used.

8. The feasibility of achieving the potential gains has not received much attention in the literature in this context. One exception is the article by Boadway (1974), which shows that even if actual transfers involve no costs, the process of compensation itself may change the relative prices facing consumers and producers. In that case, merely having $\sum \mathrm{CV} > 0$ does not guarantee that gainers can in fact compensate losers and still be better off. That is, while $\sum \mathrm{CV} > 0$ is a necessary condition for the satisfaction of the Kaldor test, it is not a sufficient one. See also Smith and Stephen (1975).

9. Atkinson (1970) has suggested, in a different context, one way of separating "efficiency" from "equity" issues. For any given real income, however distributed, compute that value of real income which, if equally distributed, would lead to the same social welfare. Comparisons can then be based on equally distributed real income equivalents, rather than on real income itself. It is hard to see how project evaluation can be based on such an approach. Moreover, it requires an explicit social valuation function.

Even though compensation tests are often claimed to be the foundation of traditional cost-benefit analysis, it is perhaps more sensible to interpret the traditional approach in a different way. If the gains and losses accruing to individuals are regarded as equal from the social point of view, then the $\sum$CV measure would represent actual, rather than potential, changes in welfare. While the calculations of rates of return and net present values will not differ, their meaning and significance will.

In this interpretation, the traditional approach requires a social valuation function. Thus, if social welfare, W, is a differentiable function of individual utilities, U_i, then

$$dW = \sum_i \frac{\partial W}{\partial U_i} dU_i,$$

and if private utility is a function only of own income, Y_i,

$$dW = \sum_i \frac{\partial W}{\partial U_i} \frac{\partial U_i}{\partial Y_i} dY_i$$

$$= \sum_i \omega_i dY_i.$$

The ω_i are then the social weights, indicating the marginal social value of an extra dollar to individual i. The traditional approach, in this interpretation, assumes $\omega_i = 1$ for all individuals.

The use of equal weights across individuals obviously involves interpersonal comparisons of utility, which is something that Kaldor and his followers tried to avoid. However much the traditionalists object to this idea, there is little doubt that the equal-weight form involving interpersonal comparisons is the form in which the traditional rate of return is typically understood and used. Economists do not merely present rates of return to decisionmakers on a take-it-or-leave-it basis; they use them to argue for or against projects, and when they do so they use the equal-weight form. The traditional rate of return is not a pure efficiency concept, and the common distinction between "economic" and "social" analysis is false.

Since social valuation is unavoidable if the economic criterion is to be meaningful, should one use equal or unequal weights? The case for using unequal weights can be brought out rather simply, as follows. Let the utility function of a poor person be $U_p(Y_p)$, and of a rich person, $U_r(Y_r)$. In the initial state, (U_p^0, U_r^0) is the distribution of utilities. Suppose a transfer, T, is to be made from the rich person to the poor person, the new state will now be (U_p^1, U_r^1), where $U_p^1 = U_p^1(Y_p + T)$ and $U_r^1 = U_r^1(Y_r - T)$. But unless the transfer is costless, a certain amount of income, S, will be "wasted" in the process. The valuation of this loss depends on who bears it. We assume for simplicity that it is borne by the rich person. Thus, his new utility level is

$$U_r^1 = U_r^1(Y_r - T - S).$$

The transfer will be desirable if

$$\alpha_p U_p^1 + \alpha_r U_r^1 > \alpha_p U_p^0 + \alpha_r U_r^0,$$

where α_p, α_r are the social weights on individual utilities. If T is optimal, then

$$\alpha_p [U_p^1 - U_p^0] = \alpha_r [U_r^0 - U_r^1].$$

For small changes, one can assume that the marginal private utility of income $(\partial U / \partial Y)$ is constant, say λ_p and λ_r. Then

$$\alpha_p \lambda_p T = \alpha_r \lambda_r (T + S),$$

or

$$\omega_p T = \omega_r (T + S).$$

with ω_p, ω_r as the social weights on income. Thus,

$$\frac{\omega_p}{\omega_r} = \frac{T + S}{T} > 1.$$

This shows that as long as the "deadweight" loss (S) of making a transfer is positive, either the appropriate welfare weights on income must be regarded as unequal or transfers from the rich to the poor must be regarded as undesirable. This does not depend on who bears the deadweight loss, or the excess burden, of the transfer. If it were entirely borne by the poor, the ratio ω_p/ω_r would be $T/T - S > 1$. The ratio would be greater than unity for all distributions of the excess burden.

Governments usually do not have the ability to make costless transfers to control the distribution of income.[10] If transfers from the rich to the poor are still considered desirable, a prima facie case for using unequal weights emerges. Moreover, very special assumptions are required to make the weights, ω_i, equal across individuals. One could assume that $\alpha_i = 1/\lambda_i$, but this would involve both differential valuation of private utilities and regressive weighting (since diminishing marginal utility of income implies that λ for a person varies inversely with income). Alternatively, one could assume that $\alpha_p = \alpha_r$ and $\lambda_p = \lambda_r$. The equality of the λ's would also imply their constancy, which is a rather strong assumption.

The Role of Economic Analysis

Economists, especially those outside the public bureaucracy, can and do assume a political role. Armed with the results of their analysis, they can

---

10. This is why the argument in Samuelson (1950) is trivial in the present context. He showed that one can separate efficiency and equity issues provided the government continually reallocates gains and losses in a lump-sum (or costless) manner so as to keep marginal utilities of income equal for all individuals.

lobby hard to get project decisions carried out their way. There is much to be said for political activism, especially if one respects the social valuation implicit in their work more than the views of ruling politicians.

But suppose it is desirable to leave judgments on social values to the decisionmakers, whoever they may be. The function of economic analysis would then be to provide information to the decisionmakers in an organized way and to leave it to the decisionmakers to bring in welfare judgments on such difficult issues as distribution of project benefits and costs. What is the best way of fulfilling this function?

If welfare judgments are to be made consistently across projects, welfare weights, whether equal or not, must be introduced explicitly in the economic analysis itself. This is the only procedure that will ensure consistency not only of value judgments but also of the way distributional considerations are defined. One would have to remove the many ambiguities that are typically involved in concerns such as greater equality and poverty redressal. Operational definitions will emerge and the weights will be applied to the relevant magnitudes. The welfare weights must, of course, be handed down to the economists from the top, whether or not they are developed through experimentation and mutual interaction between the analysts and the decisionmakers. This is basically the approach proposed by such authors as Dasgupta, Marglin, and Sen (1972) and Little and Mirrlees (1974).

In this approach, the social valuation function from which the welfare weights are derived is intended to be uniformly used from the early stages of project analysis. Even within an autonomous decisionmaking unit, a long sequence of project decisions must be made, not just the final "go or no go" decision. First, the preparation of the terms of reference for engineering and economic feasibility studies requires a precise understanding of the valuation system to be used ultimately—for example, whether (and which) distributional data are to be collected. Moreover, many projects are not "set in concrete" when financing arrangements are confirmed. Rather, projects are often adaptive processes—design decisions must be reviewed and revised each year during project implementation. Consequently, a decentralized system is required that incorporates the valuation function of the top-line decisionmakers.[11] In this sense, the process must be "top-down," although the choice of such parameters as welfare weights cannot probably be made with much conviction except through a trial-and-error process involving feedback from lower levels and a careful assessment of the implications of using the weights initially chosen. In this sense, the process could also perhaps be described as "bottom-up."

---

11. Although it is no doubt very helpful to provide sensitivity tests on distribution weights (as well as on other critical parameters, including shadow prices) at the time the final financing decision is sought, the need for a firm judgment on the specific weights to be used cannot be avoided by such means.

It is easily seen that alternative ways of bringing in social valuation do not permit consistency. Suppose, for example, that the decisionmakers are presented with an economic rate of return of 8 percent, when the test rate of discount is 10 percent, supplemented by a distributional impact statement. If now the 2 percent shortfall is overlooked because of a positive distributional impact, gross inconsistencies can result. The 2 percent shortfall may correspond to a loss (in terms of net present value) of $100,000 in one project and $10 million in another project, since rates of return need not vary with the size of projects. This problem can be avoided only if the same dollar value is assigned to each unit of the same benefit (or cost). But even this would be inadequate since such benefits and costs will occur over time—they would need to be discounted for comparisons across projects. The concept of the discount rate itself may need to be adjusted. But doing all this correctly is nothing short of integrating welfare weights into the economic analysis.

It has also been suggested that distributional concerns should be treated as constraints on project design rather than incorporated into economic analysis (Balassa, 1977). It is indeed common practice to target projects toward selected poverty groups or to design projects to minimize adverse effects on such groups. There are two reasons this approach does not permit consistency. First, projects that directly benefit the poor are only superficially different from those which do so indirectly. Second, there remains the question of how much "efficiency" costs are worth incurring to attain the specific poverty redressal or distributional objectives. In other words, the choice of constraints or targets depends on implicit valuation. This approach not only introduces inconsistency across projects, but also in the sequence of decisions within a project itself. The Appendix shows how the use of distributional concerns at the development stage and their neglect at the final stage can lead to directly contradictory judgments.

There are other ways in which the traditional form of analysis prevents decisionmakers from making welfare judgments on a consistent basis. Presenting them with the $\sum cv$ measure does not help since differential weighting requires disaggregation. Moreover, when the decision issue arrives at the desk of the decisionmaker, many important decisions have already been made. By making ad hoc judgments unavoidable, the end result may well be worse than otherwise, even from the traditionalists' point of view.

Similar issues arise with other concerns, such as basic needs, regional balance, environment, human lives, and women's participation. Should one, following the logic above, broaden economic analysis to treat such concerns systematically? Attempts to do so are rare in the literature.[12] As

---

12. The inclusion of multiple objectives has, of course, been discussed extensively in general terms; see, for example, Marglin (1967). Little and Mirrlees (1974) have also considered the inclusion of special weights on industrial employment and on regional effects.

an illustration, consider the issue of regional balance. It is not uncommon for decisionmakers and planners to introduce special regional preferences when deciding the location of projects. Two questions arise. First, what exactly is the concept? Locating an industry in a particular region does not necessarily imply that the benefits will largely accrue to the people in that region or that the disadvantaged groups within that region will receive a large share of whatever benefits do accrue. Is the regional preference one for greater economic equality or less poverty, or is some other purely locational factor involved? Second, given the definition, the question arises as to how widely the regional preference factor need be used.

Whether regional balance, or other considerations, should be incorporated in the economic analysis is a matter of trading off the benefits from greater consistency in decisionmaking against the greater complexity and inconvenience that might be involved in doing so. This tradeoff must also be faced by those who advocate the use of unequal welfare weights, since the analysis becomes more complex than with the use of equal weights. Much depends on whether the consideration is pervasive or whether it mainly arises in special cases (highway safety). The case for introducing variable welfare weights rests on the fact that if distributional or poverty concerns are strong, they are likely to bear generally on the entire spectrum of public sector projects and policies.

In numerous situations and institutional environments in both developed and developing countries, the systematic use of good economic analysis in any form is too much to hope for. In such cases, it is likely to be more sensible to introduce methods and criteria that are imperfect, perhaps highly imperfect, but that nonetheless would improve the probability of arriving at good project decisions. Sometimes even the use of the internal financial rate of return, with a minimum of adjustments to correct for the most easily identifiable distortions, can yield a better batting average than the continuation of existing practices or futile attempts at sophisticated forms of economic analysis. The use of ad hoc adjustments to reflect distributional or other considerations may be unavoidable in such contexts. Nonetheless, in inventing shortcuts and rules of thumb, one must have a clear idea of the desired form of analysis.

As distinct from problems of implementing good analysis, there might also be problems with the decisionmaking processes within the public sector. The decisionmaking apparatus of the public sector often involves a multiplicity of agencies and ministries with varying degrees of autonomy and with complex and even volatile relations with each other. The institutional features of the public sector can therefore impose severe constraints on consistency of choice and consistency in the use of those shadow prices which should be constant across projects. While such problems tend to reduce the value of cost-benefit analysis in any form, they do bear heavily on the use of unequal welfare weights. However desirable it might be in principle to use variable weights, no one recommends that each agency or each project analyst be free to choose them. Like the test rate of discount, consistency across projects cannot be compromised.

Appendix. Controlling Tradeoffs: "Hybrid" Criteria

This chapter has suggested that variable weights can be used to introduce consistency in the way economic gains in efficiency are traded off for other benefits. It is commonly thought, however, that the control of tradeoffs will require special criteria even if variable weights are used. Thus, although variable weights might be used to compare mutually exclusive options in the development stage of a project, the final acceptance of the project might be judged solely by the traditional approach. This is one example of several types of "hybrid" criteria that can be developed (Harberger, 1978).

To assess this suggestion, suppose that a one-year project is being evaluated in two steps. In the first step, one version of it (option A) is being compared with a competing version (option B). The incremental benefits and costs of A, in relation to B, all occur in one year (both are one-year project options); A's costs are − 9 and its benefits are + 7, both in efficiency terms. Suppose, also, that all costs, and six units of benefits, affect the average income group with a distribution weight of 1, but one unit of benefits accrues to a poor group with a weight of 4. Using this weight,[13] option A will be chosen according to the hybrid criterion being used, even though its net efficiency benefits are − 2.

In the second step, option A is compared with the option of doing without the project altogether, using the traditional efficiency criterion A's costs and benefits are now assumed to be − 10 and + 9 respectively. It is assumed, once again, that all but one unit of the benefits have a weight of unity, but that one unit has a weight of 4. The project is now unacceptable since the efficiency net benefits are − 1, despite the fact that the weighted value of net benefits is + 2. In rejecting this project, it is now being asserted that the weight appropriate to the poor group must be less than 2, in direct contradiction of the judgment used earlier in choosing A over B.

The hybrid criterion does not, therefore, permit consistency in treating tradeoffs. The same weight should clearly be used throughout. If the weight of 4 is considered far too high, then the appropriate procedure is to avoid excessive "waste" in terms of efficiency by choosing a lower weight. Once this is done, there is no need to invent hybrid criteria.

---

13. For example, on the grounds that it costs four units of benefits to the average group to transfer one unit to the poor group by alternative means, such as taxation.

The reader may wonder why it is necessary to discuss such hybrid criteria at all—why not dismiss them out of hand as being obviously illogical? A formal proposal to use a hybrid criterion would no doubt receive a summary dismissal. But the use of hybrid criteria, such as the one discussed above, dominates practice. It is not at all unusual to introduce distributional considerations (informally) in developing projects and then to disregard them in the final acceptance-rejection stage.

CHAPTER 3
Social Valuation

IT HAS BEEN ARGUED IN THE PREVIOUS CHAPTER that economic analysis of projects, even in its traditional form, requires a social valuation function to be meaningful. There are, however, numerous ways in which a social valuation function can be specified for constructing welfare criteria by which projects and policies can be judged. The foundation of welfare economics is indeed fluid, and it is best to be explicit about this fact of life rather than to claim consensus, passive or active, for any particular approach.[1]

It is possible, of course, to restrict in general terms the types of valuation functions that can be considered if distributional issues are at all to be introduced. It is well known that individual orderings of social states without cardinality and interpersonal comparability provide too narrow an informational base to allow any scope for distributional concerns. Arrow's famous "impossibility theorem" was developed in such a framework. One cannot say in that framework that a person gains more in moving from state X to Y than from state Z to W, nor can one say that one individual is better or worse off than another in a given state. In fact, the concepts of "rich" and "poor" persons cannot be defined in such a limited framework.

To allow scope for distributional concerns, one must permit interpersonal comparability, with or without cardinality. If interpersonal comparability is introduced without cardinality, it is possible to base distributional judgments on relative levels of well-being of different persons, but not on considerations of relative gains and losses. The rank-order method of Sen (1976) is an example. Interpersonal comparability with cardinality is required if one does not wish to impose any limitations in introducing distributional concerns (see Sen, 1974).

While it may be desirable to choose a cardinal valuation function with full comparability (whereby both levels and changes in individual welfare can be compared), the set of rules with that feature is large. The approach most commonly used in the recent literature imposes four additional restrictions: additive separability, symmetry, strict concavity, and constant elasticity of marginal utility. Symmetry is a mild condition,[2] strict concavity

---

1. For a review of the foundations of welfare economics, see Sen (1979).
2. However, if welfare of an individual is defined as a function of his income alone, then the assumption of symmetry becomes less defensible. Nonsymmetry may then be needed to allow for factors other than income, such as leisure differences.

is needed for egalitarianism, and additive separability and the constant-elasticity assumptions might be justifiable on the grounds of simplicity and convenience. This approach does, however, have the advantage of being more general than the approach used in traditional cost-benefit analysis.

The Constant-Elasticity Form

The constant-elasticity form of the social valuation function is:

$$W = \sum_{i=1}^{n} \frac{1}{\alpha}(U_i)^\alpha, \quad \alpha \neq 0, U_i > 0. \tag{3.1}$$

The function W is Paretian since

$$W_i' \equiv \frac{\partial W}{\partial U_i} = U_i^{\alpha-1} > 0.$$

It is strictly concave if $\alpha < 1$, since

$$W_i'' \equiv \frac{\partial^2 W}{\partial U_i^2} = (\alpha - 1)U_i^{\alpha-2} < 0.$$

Strict concavity ensures that the marginal contribution to social welfare diminishes as a person's utility increases, and thus an "aversion" to inequality in individual utilities is built in. When $\alpha = 1$, the form reduces to the classical utilitarian one, which is indifferent to inequality in individual utility levels (see Sen, 1973).

The elasticity of marginal social welfare of individual utilities in this case is

$$-U_i \frac{W_i''}{W_i'} = 1 - \alpha = m. \tag{3.2}$$

The social valuation function, W, therefore, has a constant elasticity parameter.

The relative welfare weights for persons i and j can be derived simply as

$$h_{ij} = W_i'/W_j'$$
$$= (U_i/U_j)^{\alpha-1}$$
$$= (U_j/U_i)^m. \tag{3.3}$$

This formulation relates the welfare weights to the levels of individual utilities, U_i. For operational purposes we must also specify forms for U_i in terms of observable parameters, such as income. The usual practice is to relate U_i to income (or consumption), assuming a constant elasticity of the private marginal utility of income (or consumption). If this parameter is ε_i, and if income is Y_i, then

$$U_i = \frac{1}{1 - \varepsilon_i} Y_i^{1 - \varepsilon_i}. \qquad (3.4)$$

The value of ε_i is restricted to $0 \le \varepsilon_i < 1$ in order to assure positive U_i. With this definition,

$$U_i' = Y_i^{-\varepsilon_i} > 0.$$

The relative income weights for persons i and j are given by

$$g_{ij} = U_i'/U_j'$$
$$= \frac{Y_i^{-\varepsilon_i}}{Y_j^{-\varepsilon_j}}.$$

It is common practice to simplify further by assuming $\varepsilon = \varepsilon_i = \varepsilon_j$, all i and j. The relative weights are then

$$g_{ij} = (Y_j/Y_i)^\varepsilon. \qquad (3.5)$$

We still need to derive the relative weights in terms of the differential effects of income on social welfare. The social weights are, using equations (3.3) and (3.5), and defining $W_{iy}' \equiv \partial W/\partial Y_i$,

$$d_{ij} = W_{iy}'/W_{jy}'$$
$$= (U_j/U_i)^m (Y_j/Y_i)^\varepsilon$$
$$= h_{ij} g_{ij}.$$

Using equation (3.4), we can substitute the utility levels and express d_{ij} as:

$$d_{ij} = (Y_j/Y_i)^{m(1 - \varepsilon)} (Y_j/Y_i)^\varepsilon$$
$$= (Y_j/Y_i)^{m(1 - \varepsilon) + \varepsilon}. \qquad (3.6)$$

The relative social weights will, therefore, depend on two elasticity parameters: m and ε. Only if the utilitarian social welfare function is chosen, the relative weights will depend on ε alone (since $\alpha = 1$ implies $m = 0$). It is conventional, however, to relate the social weights to another elasticity parameter—the elasticity of the social marginal welfare of individual income. This is assumed to be the same for every person's income and is defined as

$$\eta \equiv - Y_i W_{iy}''/W_{iy}'.$$

It can be shown that if $0 < \varepsilon < 1$,[3]

$$\eta = m(1 - \varepsilon) + \varepsilon \qquad (3.7a)$$

---

3. See Anand (1973), Balassa (1977), and Stern (1977a). Simply use equations (3.1) and (3.4), develop expressions for the first and second partials of W with respect to income, and use the

and if $\varepsilon > 1$,

$$\eta = m(\varepsilon - 1) + \varepsilon. \tag{3.7b}$$

Thus, using equations (3.6) and (3.7a), the social weights can be written simply as[4]

$$d_{ij} = (Y_j/Y_i)^\eta. \tag{3.8}$$

This approach therefore yields a very simple formula for deriving relative weights. One chooses any convenient income level as the numeraire, say, the per capita income level in the country concerned. The weight d is then a hyperbolic function of the income level Y_i, with a value of unity at the per capita income level ($\bar{Y}$). This is illustrated in Figure 1.

Some special cases are:

- Given the definition of $W, m = 0$ implies $\varepsilon = \eta$, and $W = \sum_i U_i$, which is the classical utilitarian form. It is not egalitarian in utility levels, even though the marginal social valuation of income still implies diminishing relative weights as income increases. That is, $d_{ij} = (Y_j/Y_i)^\eta$, and η can be large or small.
- If $m = 0 = \varepsilon$, then $\eta = 0$, and $W = \sum_i Y_i$. In that case, all weights are unity (the vertical line in Figure 1).
- If $m \to \infty$, the Rawlsian maximin rule is obtained, namely, $W = \text{Min}_i\{U_i\}$. The objective then is to maximize the utility of the worst-off individual.

The first special case (utilitarianism) discussed above represents the approach taken by some authors, such as Squire and van der Tak (1975). They assume a utilitarian welfare function with identical utility functions for all individuals, defined over consumption (C) in an iso-elastic manner. Thus,

$$W = \sum_i U(C_i),$$

with

$$U_i' > 0 \text{ and } U_i'' < 0,$$

and

$$U(C_i) = \frac{C_i^{1-\eta}}{1-\eta}, \quad \eta \neq 1$$

$$= \log C_i, \quad \eta = 1.$$

---

definitions of η, m, and ε. When $\varepsilon > 1$, the welfare function must, however, be rewritten to derive equation (3.7b), as

$$W = -[1/(1+m)] \sum_{i=1}^{n} [-U(Y_i)]^{1+m}.$$

4. The same formula applies when $\varepsilon > 0$. When the utility levels are restricted to negative values, the W form to be used is as shown in note 3.

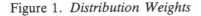

Figure 1. *Distribution Weights*

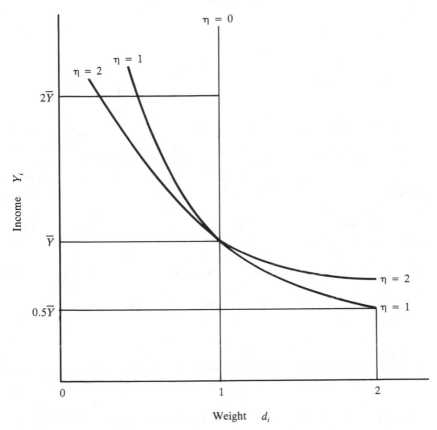

The private and the social elasticities are the same in this approach, that is, $\eta = \varepsilon$. While this approach is not egalitarian in utility levels ($\alpha = 1$), the assumption that all individuals have identical utility functions makes it so in terms of consumption levels.[5] Thus, if costless transfers were feasible across the board, the optimal distribution would involve complete equality in both utility and consumption levels.

The basic approach discussed thus far consists of two steps. First, individual utility is defined as a concave transform on individual income or consumption levels, assuming identical utility functions (this restriction can, of course, be relaxed at the expense of simplicity); second, social welfare is defined as another concave transform of individual utilities (or linear as in

5. The additively separable welfare function for a continuous distribution can be written as $W = \int_0 U(C) f(C) dC$.

the Squire–van der Tak case mentioned above). While the second step clearly depends on the ethical values of whoever defines it, the reasonableness of the first step does raise the question of whether the utility functions are realistic.

The question of realism in this respect is, however, a very difficult one. There have been many attempts to estimate the elasticity of the private marginal utility of income (ε) on the basis of actual consumer behavior. The estimates, which are extensively reviewed in Stern (1977a), indicate that values of ε between, say, 1 and 3, are not unreasonable as orders of magnitude, but neither the evidence nor the methodologies applied encourage great confidence. For example, the econometric demand studies which yield such estimates assume additively separable utility functions. The empirical validity of this assumption can be challenged, especially when used in complete demand systems. Moreover, the estimated elasticities will change for any monotonic transformation of the utility functions used which give rise to the same demand system.[6]

It is therefore difficult to see how this question of realism can be settled in practice. This relates not only to the form of the utility functions one chooses, but also to the assumption, as in Squire and van der Tak (1975), that all such functions are identical. Authors, such as Lal (1980), who cite realism as the basis for their choices of ε, say a "central" value of 2 with reference to the work of Stern (1977a), perhaps claim too much.[7]

An important feature of the constant-elasticity form is that the weights, d_i, tend to become very large as income disparities increase. Thus, if the distribution of income in a country is very unequal, the weights applicable to the poorest segments will be extremely high. For example, if a person's income is one-tenth the average level, his marginal gains will be weighted by 10 if $\eta = 1$, and by 100 if $\eta = 2$. Is it conceivable that suitable transfer programs cannot be designed by the government to achieve much greater equality when the benefits of doing so are assumed to be so great?

One can note, to begin with, that the effective weights in the analysis are not d_i, but d_i/v, where v is the shadow price of public income compared with the value of consumption gains to someone at the average income level (see Chapter 5). This shadow price should depend also on η. Thus, if $\eta = 3$, there will be very high pay-offs from using public expenditures for poverty redressal, and v should therefore have a high value also. Thus, the effective weight, d_i/v, will be much less than the unadjusted weight, d_i, at any income level. The combined use of a relatively low value of v, say 3, and a relatively high value for η, say also 3, is not therefore proper, unless one assumes that

---

6. These points are discussed in detail in chapter five of Deaton and Muellbauer (1980).

7. Whatever realism there is in such a choice of ε, it is the value of η that is really wanted. Whether one assumes $\eta = \varepsilon$, as in Squire and van der Tak (1975), or $\varepsilon + 1 = \eta$, as in Lal (1980), one is essentially performing an arbitrary operation.

the government will not in fact pursue significant poverty redressal programs despite their high social pay-offs. But that assumption would make the use of a high value of η questionable. Of course, if one could observe a unique value of the private elasticity (ε), then one could also have a basis for insisting that $\varepsilon < \eta$, and perhaps for proceeding to draw up an ambitious poverty redressal program. But, as earlier discussed, it is difficult to insist on a unique and observable ε.

One might also argue in the following ways:

- If the income disparities in a country are not great, then d_i/v may not be large even if $\eta = 2$ or 3.
- Although the government would like large-scale poverty redressal programs, it is unable, for political reasons, to pursue them through means other than investment projects.
- The costs of poverty-redressal programs increase rapidly with the size of such programs, and therefore even very high values of d_i/v are not enough to justify large-scale programs needed to reduce income disparities significantly and quickly.

All these are empirically testable arguments, and one should therefore look into these issues before selecting a value for η, or before selecting the constant-elasticity form itself. At any rate, it seems unwise to choose a value for η without first checking its reasonableness, as several authors have done. Alternatively, one could modify the weighting system by setting upper and lower bounds on the weights while retaining the constant-elasticity form within those limits.

The Traditional Approach

The traditional practice of measuring gains as the equally weighted sum of producer and consumer surpluses can be represented by the second special case discussed above, namely, $m = \eta = \varepsilon = 0$, implying, with Y_i as incomes,

$$W = \sum_i U_i = \sum_i Y_i.$$

More generally, the traditional form is consistent with an indirect utility function, defined on the price and income space, as follows:

$$V_i = A_i(\bar{p}) + \beta(\bar{p}) Y_i,$$

where A_i and β depend on the price vector ($\bar{p}$) only. Thus, social welfare can be written in the indirect form as $V(\sum_i Y_i, \bar{p})$. Note that the parameter β is the marginal (private) utility of income and is assumed to be the same for all individuals (this also implies that it must be constant).

It follows from Roy's identity ($x_i^j = -\partial U_j/\partial p_i/\partial U_j/\partial Y_j$) that the Marshallian demand function of person j for good x_i must be of the form

$$x_i^j = -a(\bar{p}) + b(\bar{p})Y_j.$$

In other words, all Engel curves must be linear. The traditional form in this interpretation implies acceptance of a strong assumption regarding preferences for which no factual or intuitive presumption exists. Some authors, however, suggest that this assumption is likely to be reasonable for evaluating small changes. But projects often create large changes, both in prices and incomes.

The Introduction of Leisure

Thus far, the weights have been related to measured consumption, with no explicit reference to leisure. If leisure is treated as a consumption good, then the relative weights will, in general, depend on both individual consumption and leisure levels. Leisure can be ignored in defining the weights only if it is excluded from the social valuation function, or if the social valuation function is separable in consumption and leisure.

Consider the utilitarian function:

$$W = \sum_i U(C_i, L_i),$$

where L_i represents leisure, with

$$U(C_i, L_i) = \frac{1}{1-\eta}[C_i + g(L_i)]^{1-\eta}, \quad \eta \geq 0, \eta \neq 1$$
$$= \log[C_i + g(L_i)], \quad \eta = 1.$$

Then

$$\frac{\partial W}{\partial C_i} = [C_i + g(L_i)]^{-\eta}.$$

Therefore, the relative weights will depend also on L_i, that is,

$$\frac{d_i}{d_j} = \frac{[C_i + g(L_i)]^{-\eta}}{[C_j + g(L_j)]^{-\eta}}.$$

This problem does not arise if $\eta = 0$, as in the traditional approach. In that case,

$$U(C_i, L_i) = aC_i + g(L_i),$$

and, given the utilitarian W function,

$$\frac{\partial W}{\partial C_i} = a = \frac{\partial W}{\partial C_j}.$$

Thus, $d_i = d_j = 1$.

Some authors have suggested that governments should wish to value leisure less than individuals do.[8] The treatment of leisure in that fashion is analogous, from the analytical point of view, to the basic needs approach discussed below. The valuation of leisure is further discussed in the Appendix.

The Basic Needs Approach

An alternative to the approaches discussed above is to retain the equal weighting rule of the traditional approach, while introducing special weights on the consumption of specific commodities by the poor. In principle, such weights can be derived from the notion of consumption externalities—the fact that additional consumption of certain types of goods by the poor may make the nonpoor happier and the latter may therefore be willing to subsidize the poor (see Harberger, 1978b).

It is not possible to measure the willingness of the nonpoor to pay for the external benefits they receive from poverty redressal, and even if it were, the question of whether their altruistic instincts are sufficiently strong cannot be really avoided. Paternalism will necessarily be involved in the selection of the commodities for special treatment as well as in the definitions of the consumption standards by which deprivation is to be measured. This approach will also therefore involve exogenous judgments of the policymakers. Nonetheless, it may be easier to agree on a set of basic needs and on social norms regarding adequate consumption levels than on distribution weights.

The paper by Scandizzo and Knudsen (1980) is a good illustration of this approach. Suppose that food, measured in terms of caloric intake, is chosen as a basic-need good, and a social norm for adequate consumption is available. Their method can then be used to evaluate the benefits of a project that increases incomes of different groups by ΔY_i, as

$$\Delta W = \sum_{i}^{n} \Delta Y_i (1 + \theta_i) + \sum_{j=1+n}^{m} \Delta Y_j,$$

8. Squire and van der Tak (1975) allow for that possibility, although they do not actually recommend it.

where $\Delta Y_i, i = 1, \ldots, n$, are the income increments of deprived groups; $\Delta Y_j, j = n + 1, \ldots, m$, are the income increments of nondeprived groups; and $\theta_i, i = 1, \ldots, n$, are special income weights. These can be written as $\theta_i = c_i \cdot w_i / p$, where c_i = marginal propensity to consume food of group i, p is the market price, and w_i are the welfare weights on additional quantities of food consumed.

The welfare weights, in turn, are defined as

$$w_i = p \frac{(g_i + g)}{2\pi},$$

where π is an average of the price elasticities of demand of nondeprived

Figure 2. *Income Weights and the Basic Needs Approach*

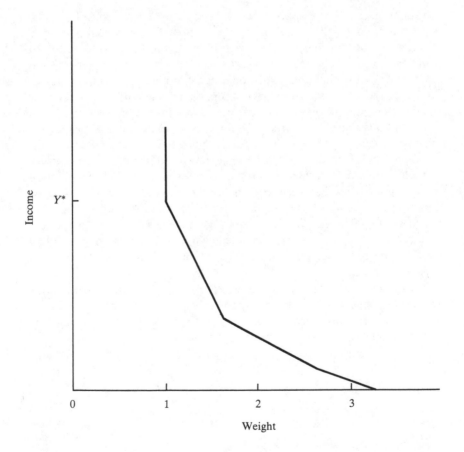

Note: Y^* is the level of income at which all basic needs are fully met. The kinks represent income thresholds at which some of the basic needs are fully met.

groups, weighted by the share of consumption of each such group in the total consumption of such groups; g_i is a measure of deprivation of group i; and g is a measure of the total deprivation suffered by all deprived groups.

The factor $(1/2\pi)(g_i + g)$ can, in principle, be very large (if π is very small). In practice, however, its value is likely to be quite low, perhaps less than 3. Consequently, the effect of weighting will be greatly dampened in relation to the use of distribution weights in the constant-elasticity form.

Nevertheless, it is readily seen that this approach, like the variable-weights approaches discussed earlier, might necessitate the use of unequal income weights quite generally in cost-benefit analysis. In fact, as the number of basic needs is increased, for example, to include basic education, minimum shelter, and potable water (why not beer also?), virtually all the expenditures of the poor will require differential weighting. Thus, one may view this approach as another way of rationalizing and defining variable income weights. The weighting function will then be similar to the one in Figure 2. But, in principle, both variable income weights and basic needs weights can logically be used simultaneously in the analysis.

CHAPTER 4

Valuation of Traded and Nontraded Goods

THE VALUATION OF TRADABLE and nontradable goods is quite straightforward in traditional practice. Elements of costs and benefits that represent foreign exchange outflows and inflows are identified, and their foreign values, defined in a foreign currency, multiplied by a shadow exchange rate (SER), instead of the official (or the actual) exchange rate (OER) ruling at the time such costs and benefits occur. The SER is typically applied to easily identifiable effects, for example, to the foreign costs of imported inputs or to the foreign values of exports (or import substitutes) produced. There is nothing in principle, of course, to suggest that indirect effects are irrelevant or unimportant. For example, if a project induces additional domestic production of a nontraded input, such as transport and electricity, it will also lead to additional imports of inputs needed for that production. Alternatively, the additional expenditures on a nontradable output produced by a project will divert (or increase) expenditures from (or to) other commodities which may be tradable. How fully such effects should be accounted for is a practical issue of how much detail one should aim for in project analysis.

More troublesome is the concept of the SER itself. It has acquired over the years several different intuitive explanations. For example, some economists relate the SER to the notion of a foreign exchange constraint, or bottleneck, that developing countries supposedly suffer from. The development literature of the 1950s did in fact often assume a negative relation between balance of payments surpluses and economic growth: if export revenues grow exogenously, and if imports depend on income, then growth must entail balance of payments difficulties.[1] Subsequently, the notion of a foreign exchange bottleneck received emphasis in the gap models of Chenery and others (see, for example, McKinnon, 1964). But in such models there is not really a foreign exchange bottleneck unless one assumes that export revenues cannot be increased by increasing the volume of exports, an unlikely assumption for any developing country. A strict foreign exchange constraint in gap models can hold only in very special cases: (1) if there are

---

1. This is not, however, necessarily true if one introduces portfolio choices between money and other assets in the model, as one should. In that case, import demand will depend on both income and the demand for money, and it can be shown that income growth may require balance of payments surpluses to maintain monetary equilibrium (see Mundell, 1968).

no opportunities for import substitution and for increasing export earnings; (2) if the import intensity of domestic production cannot be reduced; and (3) if the marginal utility of present consumption is zero. The notion of a foreign exchange constraint in such models is therefore quite misleading, since the bottleneck relates to limitations of both domestic and foreign transformation possibilities.[2]

The definition of the SER in traditional theory does not quite deal with this concern. Although its definition has changed somewhat over recent years, it is in essence defined as an average of duties and subsidies impinging on foreign trade at the margin. As such, the traditional SER should not be confused with what the actual exchange rate would be if that rate were allowed to float freely in the market, nor should it be confused with the value that the exchange rate would take if the government followed "first-best" policies throughout the economy.[3]

The treatment of shadow exchange rates in Little and Mirrless (1974), and in contributions using their method,[4] is somewhat different from the traditional approach, even if one disregards the special adjustments they make for the valuation of public income and the introduction of differential welfare weights. They express all values in foreign exchange equivalent units (their chosen numeraire), which immediately introduces a significant semantic difference. They use conversion factors to carry out the reverse transformation from domestic values to foreign exchange equivalent values, and all necessary adjustments are included in those factors. The conversion factor for any nontraded good is still, like the SER, a weighted average of price distortions; but both the weights and the price distortions will tend to differ for each nontraded good.

If one multiplies the reciprocal of a conversion factor by the official or actual exchange rate one gets an adjustment factor with the same dimensions as the SER. Consequently, the Little–Mirrlees technique is often described as one with multiple SERs, rather than a single one as in the traditional approach. Little and Mirrlees (1974, p. 354) clearly saw the matter in this way: "it is the inappropriate use of a single shadow exchange rate, or general blunderbuss, which we deprecate." Formal models that yield a single SER do indeed assume that all nontraded goods can be treated as if they were a single good, as confirmed by Blitzer, Dasgupta, and Stiglitz (1981).

This chapter deals at length with the conversion factor approach and its relation to the traditional method, leaving out the special adjustments that

2. See Findlay (1971) and Lal (1972).
3. The simplest exposition of the traditional SER is in Harberger (1977). For a more formal treatment see Blitzer, Dasgupta, and Stiglitz (1981).
4. For example, Hughes (1978), Powers (1981), Scott, MacArthur, and Newbery (1974), Squire and van der Tak (1975), and Lal (1974).

Little and Mirrlees suggest for savings and income inequality considerations (discussed in the next two chapters). A careful examination of this relation is important since it is the key to many of the recent controversies in this area. It will be seen, for example, that many of the popular criticisms of the Little–Mirrlees system are misplaced.

For example, there is no error involved in their treatment of nontraded goods, whether or not the supply functions of such goods are inelastic. As another example, it is simply not true that "the L–M system assigns to all tradable commodities accounting prices (APs) defined by their border prices, thereby rejecting domestic willingness to pay (i.e., demand prices) as a determinant of social value" (Weiscarver, 1979). As yet another example, the use of foreign exchange as the numeraire does not mean that only direct and indirect foreign exchange effects are counted—contrary to Boadway (1978). Furthermore, the so-called Little–Mirrlees rule of border pricing— that relative border prices of tradable commodities are also their relative shadow prices—is also a precept of traditional theory. In circumstances in which this precept is invalid—such as when border prices vary with a country's policies—similar adjustments are needed in both approaches.

The validity or otherwise of the border pricing rule has been examined recently by Blitzer, Dasgupta, and Stiglitz (1981), and by Bhagwati and Srinivasan (1981). Their main conclusions are simple and can be summarized as follows. Even if border prices are assumed to be exogenous, the border pricing rule breaks down if the project induces changes in distortionary trade duties or domestic indirect taxes, changes in the tariffs implicit in foreign exchange rationing, or changes in the prices of nontraded goods. Such changes affect consumer prices, and it therefore becomes necessary to take account of the effects on consumer surpluses. This is not, however, a criticism of the Little–Mirrlees framework since it can easily cope with such effects. This framework is, as explained at length in this chapter, essentially the same as the traditional "consumer plus producer surplus" or "efficiency" framework, if savings and income inequality concerns are excluded. This is perhaps brought out best in Squire and van der Tak (1975, especially pp. 142–47).

An interesting point that emerges from the article by Blitzer, Dasgupta, and Stiglitz is that one cannot rely on border pricing alone if foreign borrowing is nonoptimal. In that case, the traditional efficiency framework breaks down. One then must use the *full* Little–Mirrlees method, including a premium on public income, as discussed in Chapters 5 and 6. To check this, simply set $\lambda = \phi$ in either equation 22 or 33 of their paper. The ratio of these parameters, λ/ϕ, is in fact the shadow price of public income, or s in the Little–Mirrlees method. As they themselves point out, the adjustments they suggest are the same as those required in the full Little–Mirrlees method.

Since the adjustments for savings and income inequality are excluded from this chapter, the discussion should enable the reader to compare the

Little–Mirrlees approach more easily with the traditional approach. Issues are clearer if separated in this way. It is also highly convenient in practice first to compute conversion factors without savings or inequality effects and then to adjust them, as and when necessary and feasible, as a second step. Some authors include the savings factor only in the second step, describing the conversion factors thus derived as "extended efficiency conversion factors," and then add another step if income distribution weights are also needed. All-inclusive conversion factors, called "social conversion factors," are discussed in Chapter 6.

The next section discusses efficiency conversion factors and their relation to shadow exchange rates, the approximations frequently used in practice, and some common estimation procedures. Conversion factors are sensitive to changes in trade policy, and their estimates typically reflect the current trade regime and only those policy changes that can be confidently forecast for the near term. It is often very difficult to use a longer-term perspective, as in the case of many other parameters required for project analysis—for example, domestic and foreign inflation rates and movements in the actual currency exchange rates. The final section indicates a possible way of simplifying problems in evaluating projects in situations of external imbalance. Appendix A briefly examines the relation between the conversion factor approach and the "domestic resource cost" method, which is a variant of the traditional approach commonly used in general studies of resource allocation. Appendix B provides a summary of some of the main conversion factor formulas.

The Conversion Factor Approach

This section reviews standard practice in the conversion factor approach. First, conversion factors are defined, with emphasis on their relation to shadow exchange rates. Then commodity-specific and aggregate conversion factors are discussed. Finally, some common methods of estimating aggregate conversion factors are explained.

Conversion factors and shadow exchange rates

In a project in which nontraded goods and services are not involved, or are negligible, the SER has no role to play, although the project may have significant effects on the balance of payments. If the project—for example, an enclave mining project—produces US$$X$ of exports (valued in FOB prices), and uses US$$M$ of imports (in CIF prices), with few or no nontraded inputs, the valuation of the project will depend only on whether the annual net benefits $(X - M)$ produce a positive present value or not. The net benefits of the project, thus measured, may be large, with significant effects on the country's balance of payments and foreign exchange reserves, but such effects cannot be taken into account by using an SER different from the official rate.

Benefits and costs were measured in U.S. dollar units in this example. But whether these net benefits are measured in U.S. dollars or in local currency units at the official exchange rate, or in local currency units at some other exchange rate, has no bearing on the analysis, since the sign of the net present value (NPV) will not be altered. Unless otherwise indicated, all values are expressed in units of the local currency at the official exchange rate. In effect, although all values are measured in foreign exchange, their denomination is in local currency rather than in U.S. dollars or some other foreign currency. Sometimes this unit is referred to as the "border currency" unit, such as "border rupees," to emphasize the point that the values thus expressed differ from the values measured in domestic market prices. Thus, an imported good worth US$100 before duty (that is, in CIF prices) would be worth Rs1,000 in border rupees if the official exchange rate is Rs10 per US$1, and Rs1,250 in terms of domestic prices if there is a 25 percent import duty.

The SER is relevant to project analysis only if both traded and nontraded commodities are involved. To define the role of the SER better, suppose that the project involves not only $X and $M of traded outputs and inputs, respectively, but also Rs N of nontraded inputs valued in domestic market prices. The project account would, in the first instance, appear to be as follows (with Rs10 = US$1 as the official rate):

$$\text{Net benefits in Rs} = 10(X - M) - N.$$

This would not be correct, however, because the cost of the nontraded input must be adjusted so as to be correct relative to the border prices of the traded goods. The market prices of the domestic inputs may incorporate various imperfections because of noncompetitive pricing, external effects, and indirect taxes or subsidies. All these factors must be taken into account in adjusting the value of this input.

After all the necessary adjustments have been worked out, the project account can be correctly expressed as

$$\text{Net benefits in Rs} = 10(X - M) - cN,$$

where c is the overall adjustment factor that converts the market value, N, to its value in shadow prices expressed in border currency units. This adjustment factor is the general definition of a *conversion factor*.

One could write the project account by expressing all values in terms of domestic market prices. Thus:

$$\text{Net benefits in Rs} = \frac{10}{c}(X - M) - N,$$

or

$$= s(X - M) - N,$$

where $s = 10/c$.

Since all items are multiplied by a common factor $(1/c)$, the sign of the
NPV will not change and the same decision will result. The factor s, which
equals the ratio of the official rate (10 to 1) to the conversion factor c, is one
definition of the *shadow exchange rate* (SER).

This definition of the SER is comprehensive since it incorporates all the
necessary adjustments to the domestic cost, N. Usually, however, it is
defined more narrowly to include only trade-related adjustments. In that
case, the adjustments not incorporated in the SER must be allowed for
separately. If the SER is defined more narrowly, say s', and if the remaining
adjustments necessary are s'', the net benefits can be written as $(s'X - s'M$
$- s''N)$. This will yield the same result if $s'/s'' \equiv s$. There is, however, no
unique way of deciding which adjustments to include in the SER, s'. Any
definition of s' is correct as long as the factor s'' is defined correspondingly
to capture all the remaining adjustments that are necessary.

To illustrate this further, assume that the nontraded input in the example
given above is labor. Two adjustments may be necessary. First, the
domestic cost of labor, RsN, may be too high because the project wages are
set higher than the value of the output forgone. This distortion would then
require a downward adjustment of the cost of labor; if the value of the
output forgone in domestic prices is half the cost, then the adjustment factor,
c_1, would be 0.5. Second, the value of the output forgone will need further
adjustments since it will reflect duties and subsidies, and other distortionary
measures, that directly or indirectly bear on the alternative activities from
which labor is drawn. This adjustment, say c_2, may be less or greater than
unity. It would be less than unity if the labor is drawn from production of an
import substitute (rice) whose domestic price exceeds the border price
because of an import tariff—for example, c_2 would be 0.8 if Rs 100 of less
rice output (in domestic prices) would involve Rs 80 of more rice imports
(because of an import duty of 25 percent). It would be greater than unity if
labor is drawn from production of an exportable (cotton) whose domestic
price is below the border price because of an export duty—for example, c_2
would be 1.25 if Rs 100 less of cotton output (in domestic prices) would lead
to Rs 125 less of cotton exports (because of a 25 percent export duty).

The net benefits can now be written as

$$\text{Net benefits in Rs} = 10(X - M) - c_2 c_1 N,$$

or
$$= s(X - M) - N,$$

where $s = 10/(c_2 c_1)$; or alternatively as

$$= s'(X - M) - c_1 N,$$

where $s' = 10/c_2$. The definition of the SER (s or s') thus depends in this case
on whether only the distortions affecting the border-price valuation of
labor's forgone output (reflected in the factor c_2) are to be taken into

account or also the imperfections in the labor market itself (reflected in the factor c_1).

Since the SER is a commodity-specific concept, its definition depends first on the particular nontraded goods and services involved—the adjustments necessary for labor costs, for example, are likely to be quite different from the adjustments necessary for raw material. Second, unless all the necessary adjustments to domestic prices are included in the SER, the correct definition will depend on what other adjustments remain to be made separately.

Moreover, economists working on projects are often provided with SER estimates prepared by others. The form $s'(X - M) - c_1 N$ is then used, with c_1 representing the project and commodity-specific adjustments to be carried out by project analysts. However, as discussed above, the SER, s', cannot be defined independently of the adjustments included in c_1. The practice of estimating s' and c_1 separately, and by different persons in different contexts, is therefore liable to lead to errors.[5]

It is preferable for this reason to use instead the border pricing form $10(X - M) - cN$, with $c = c_2 c_1$. All necessary adjustments are included in the single factor c, which is clearly tied to the specific nontraded items included in N. This form focuses on the specific commodities involved and considers all interrelated adjustments jointly. In this sense, the use of the conversion factor approach has a practical advantage over approaches using shadow exchange rates.[6]

Using conversion factors

While a separate conversion factor should, in principle, be defined for each nontraded good, it is neither feasible nor necessary to do so. Averages must be used. The following discussion focuses on the main adjustments needed in project analysis to bring out the roles of both specific and average conversion factors.

Project costs, whether capital or operating, basically consist of equipment and raw materials that are, on balance, imported or exported by the

5. It may be useful to amplify the preceding illustration by considering two nontraded inputs, A and B, with conversion factors a and b, respectively. The net benefits would then be $10(X - M) - aA - bB$. If s, the SER, is now defined as $10/a$, the alternative form becomes $s(X - M) - A - cB$, with $c \equiv b/a$. The SER could also be defined as a weighted average such that $s = 10/d$, with $d = (aA + bB)/(A + B)$; in this case the correct form would be $s(X - M) - (A + B)$. However, defining s as an economywide average of domestic expenditures on a large number of goods may lead to large errors, since s does not reflect the specific considerations relevant to the project.

6. Individual conversion factors correspond to individual shadow exchange rates. Thus, if c is the conversion factor for a nontraded good, OER/c is its shadow exchange rate, OER being the official exchange rate. The ratio $1/c$ may be interpreted as the shadow price of using foreign exchange on the particular good concerned (see Dasgupta, Marglin, and Sen, 1972, pp. 215–16).

country, and nontraded items such as labor and land. The costs of the traded items (mostly imports or import substitutes), are usually a large share of total costs and are expressed directly in border prices (CIF or FOB prices at the official exchange rate). No further adjustments are required when it is reasonable to assume that the border prices are not affected by the project. When the costs of the traded items are expressed initially in domestic market prices, these must be converted to border prices by taking out duties and taxes. Thus, for any input of which the country is a net importer at a constant CIF price, the conversion factor (CF) is simply the inverse of one plus the effective duty rate t, that is,

$$CF = \frac{\text{border price}}{\text{domestic price}} = \frac{1}{1+t}.$$

Similarly, for an input procured locally at the expense of exports, the CF is simply the inverse of the export duty or subsidy, if any, that is, the inverse of $1 + \text{subsidy rate}$, or $1 - \text{duty rate}$. For simplicity, distribution and transport margins are ignored in this discussion.

The border price of an input seldom varies with the project in developing countries. If the project demand did increase the border price of an import, the relevant shadow price would no longer be its CIF price, but rather the marginal import cost, taking account of the higher price that would need to be paid on the imports that would occur without the project. The marginal import cost and marginal export revenue concepts are explained in detail in Appendix B to this chapter, equations (4.2c)–(4.2d) and (4.2e)–(4.2g).[7]

Projects typically include many nontradable items. There may also be cases in which an input is tradable but because of quotas or other forms of quantitative restrictions is not traded at the margin. In such cases, the project demand for the input must be met by either expanding domestic production or by curtailing its use by others, or partly by both.

The main consideration in such cases is whether the price of the input is independent of the project or whether the project demand increases it. The common practice is to assume price constancy unless there is clear evidence to the contrary. When this assumption is justified, the market price equals the supply price and the appropriate conversion factors for nontraded goods are derived entirely from data on costs of production.

When the supply price is the relevant one, the production costs can be decomposed, step by step, into traded and nontraded elements. Thus, highway transport costs can be decomposed into vehicle costs, fuel costs,

---

7. In practice, one should carry out a full analysis of the changes in import expenditures (or export revenues), in tax revenues, and in domestic consumer and producer surpluses. As Appendix B makes clear, the use of the marginal import cost or the marginal export revenue concepts is valid only in special cases. See also Bhagwati and Srinivasan (1981) for a formal discussion of project evaluation with variable border prices.

repair costs, drivers' wages, and so on. At each step, the traded elements can be directly evaluated in terms of border prices and the nontraded items further disaggregated. The number of desirable decomposition steps depends on the importance of the nontraded input in total project costs, and the importance of the nontraded residual in the cost of the nontraded input. Experience indicates that even when the nontraded input is important in total costs, it is rarely desirable to carry out more than two or three steps in the decomposition process. This process can be represented as follows: If C is total cost in market prices of the input, consisting of subitems $C_1, C_2, \ldots$, with corresponding conversion factors, $c, c_1, c_2, \ldots$, then

$$cC = c_1 C_1 + c_2 C_2 + c_3 C_3 + \ldots,$$

or $\qquad c = c_1(C_1/C) + c_2(C_2/C) + c_3(C_3/C) + \ldots.$

The overall conversion factor will be insensitive to any subitem with a small share in total costs. Such conversion factors, based on production cost data, may be called supply-price conversion factors.

In contrast, there may occasionally be cases in which the supply of an input is completely fixed, additional project demand being met at the expense of other domestic uses of that input. Such cases may arise when land to be used in a project is available only in limited amounts or when the input is entirely imported with a strict quota that is fully utilized by others.[8] Such cases may also be relevant when the production of the input is subject to strict capacity constraints—peak period electricity—which cannot be broken in the short run. With completely inelastic supply, the market clearing price would be independent of production costs and set by demand factors alone. The opportunity cost of using the input in the project would now be its demand price, from which the conversion factor must be derived. To find the conversion factor, it is necessary to study the demand pattern of other users. As a simple illustration, assume that the project input is electric power and that the project demand would be met at the expense of users who would now switch (because of the higher effective price of electricity) to substitutes such as gas and kerosene. If the diverted expenditure is distributed to gas (60 percent), kerosene (30 percent), and other products (10 percent), with conversion factors 0.5 for gas (indicating that the cost in border prices is half the domestic gas price), 1.8 for kerosene (indicating a subsidy on kerosene imports), and 0.8 for others (a weighted average factor for the other goods), the demand-price conversion factor for electric power can be estimated as $0.5(0.6) + 1.8(0.3) + 0.8(0.1) = 0.92$. In effect, this indicates that for every Rs100 of expenditures switched to electricity substitutes, Rs92 of foreign exchange costs are incurred.

---

8. Quotas and other forms of quantitative restrictions tend to be applied on an ad hoc basis, exemptions being allowed in special cases, such as meeting the project input requirements. In the presence of exemptions, quotas should, of course, be disregarded in project analysis.

In between the two extremes of perfectly elastic and perfectly inelastic supply is the intermediate case, that is, when additional project demand is met partly from additional domestic production and partly at the expense of other domestic uses. The market price would then be somewhere between the supply and demand prices defined above. In this intermediate case, the conversion factor is a weighted average of the supply- and demand-price conversion factors, the weights being the elasticities of supply and demand. The formula, discussed in more detail in Appendix B, is

$$CF = \frac{\alpha E + \beta N}{E + N},$$

where α and β are the supply- and demand-price conversion factors, and E and N are the (absolute) values of the supply- and demand-price elasticities. If the elasticities are equal, then the CF is the arithmetic average of the two conversion factors. If the supply elasticity is much higher than the demand elasticity, then the CF approximates α, the supply-price conversion factor. This is the assumption most commonly made in practice. The general approach, however, is similar to that discussed in Harberger (1977).

For project outputs that are exported or that substitute perfectly for imports, valuation is directly based on border prices. But for certain commodities such as tea, cocoa, rubber, rice, sugar, and coffee, the assumption that border prices are not affected by the output from the project is not always reasonable. For exports subject to inelastic demand, the correct price in project evaluation is not the FOB price. With complete specialization, the correct price is the marginal export revenue, which is lower than the FOB price. If, in a particular case, the existing export duty on such an export is regarded as optimal, the shadow price would equal the FOB price net of the duty, that is, the producer price (see Appendix B, equations 4.2a to 4.2g).

In the case of nontraded ouputs, the evaluation process depends on whether their prices are affected by the project. If prices are unchanged, the gross benefits of the project will consist of incremental sales revenues alone. Increased domestic sales revenues are converted to the border price basis by the method for deriving the demand-price conversion factor discussed above. That is, since the increased expenditures on the project output are diverted from expenditures on related products, the appropriate conversion factor should be derived from the conversion factors for those products, weighted by their shares in the total expenditures diverted. In other words, increased sales revenues release real resources elsewhere. The ratio of the real resources thus released (valued in border prices) to the increase in domestic sales revenues is the appropriate conversion factor.

As another illustration, consider the valuation of increased production of sorghum, which is a nontraded food grain in some countries. Increased expenditures on sorghum, representing the sales revenues attributable to the project, might be diverted mostly from purchases of other food grains, such as rice and maize. Assume that rice is an imported product with an effective duty of 50 percent and maize is an exported product with a duty of 20 percent. For each rupee of rice demand diverted to sorghum, import needs are reduced by half a rupee (in border prices), and for each rupee of maize demand diverted to sorghum, exports are increased by Rs1.25 (in border prices). The conversion factor for valuing increased sales of sorghum is simply an average of 0.5 and 1.25, the weights being the shares of rice and maize in the marginal expenditures involved. It is naturally better to use such specific conversion factors than to use economywide aggregates, such as the general SER, which are weighted averages of a wide range of goods, most of which are only weakly related, if at all, to the project outputs in question.

The demand-price conversion factor thus reflects the pattern of demand of the users of the project output and distortions in the markets for the most closely related substitutes and complements. If the close substitutes of the project output are heavily subsidized (close complements heavily taxed), the conversion factor will tend to exceed unity, and the value of the output in shadow prices will tend to be higher than in market prices. Conversely, if the close substitutes are heavily taxed (or close complements heavily subsidized), the value of the output in shadow prices will be less than in market prices. The detailed analysis of market demand from this point of view is, however, difficult to construct and is therefore frequently the weakest part of project economic work.

If the prices of nontraded outputs fall, compared with what they would have been without the project, the evaluation of the project must include comparison of the gains received by the users with the losses on intramarginal (or "without project") production suffered by other producers. Since the losses and gains to different parties are equally weighted in traditional analysis, the intramarginal gains and losses would cancel out. The project benefits would then consist of (1) the willingness of the users to pay for the incremental project output less what they actually pay (the "triangle" measure of "consumer surplus") and (2) the expenditures on the project output.

The adjustments necessary for (2) have already been discussed. The adjustments for (1) depend on whether the outputs are final consumption goods or are intermediate goods. If this part represents an increase in consumer welfare directly, the conversion factor for expressing the welfare change in border prices should be derived from the expenditures patterns and prices relevant to the consumers involved. In practice, an overall consumption conversion factor (CCF), based on the expenditures of the average consumer, is often used as a proxy for this purpose. If, however, the surplus accrues to industrial users who use the project outputs as their inputs, then the appropriate conversion factor will reflect the conversion factors of the outputs produced by those industries and of other inputs used in the production process.

A comparative summary

The emphasis on border prices in the Little–Mirrlees technique, and especially on supply-price conversion factors, has led many to believe that domestic prices, and the traditional market-price-based willingness-to-pay concept are disregarded in that technique (see Weiscarver, 1979). To ensure that semantic differences do not mislead, and to summarize the preceding discussion more formally, a description is given below of how the same analytical steps can be represented by using different terminologies.

Case 1. Consider a product (X) that is exported at a constant FOB price. Its production requires imports (M), available at constant CIF prices, and inputs of a nontraded good (N).

In traditional practice, the net benefits (B_1) would be written as $B_1 = (\text{SER})X - (\text{SER})M - aN$, where SER is an economywide shadow exchange rate (so many rupees per dollar), and a is a factor that corrects the domestic market price of N—for example, takes out sales taxes when the market price is constant.

In the border-pricing procedure, the expression would be $B_2 = (\text{OER})X - (\text{OER})M - bN$, where OER is the actual exchange rate, and b is a conversion factor that converts the domestic price of N to the border price equivalent. The two procedures will lead to the same result if $b = a(\text{SCF})$, where SCF is a "standard" conversion factor, defined as OER/SER.

Case 2. Suppose the project increases the supply of a nontraded good such as power, but the market price of that good is not affected. The incremental revenues owing to the project are R; it is assumed to require inputs of M and N as in Case 1.

The net benefits in domestic prices would be written as $B_1 = R - (\text{SER})M - aN$.

The net benefits in border prices would be written as $B_2 = rR - (\text{OER})M - bN$, where r is the demand-price conversion factor relevant to the type of output involved. The term rR is the foreign exchange released when expenditures on other products are reduced by the amount R (in other words, the production of any output, whether directly traded or not, "earns" or "saves" foreign exchange).

The two expressions will be equivalent if instead of a specific demand-price conversion factor, r, the standard conversion factor SCF is used, with $b = a(\text{SCF})$ as before.

Case 3. This is the same as Case 2 above, but it is now assumed that the price of the nontraded output is lower with the project than without the

Figure 3. *Evaluation of a Price Change*

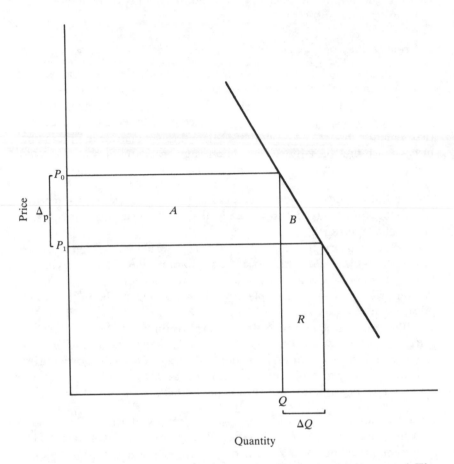

Quantity

project. It is assumed also that the output is a final consumption good. The familiar diagram for this case is shown in Figure 3.

When the price falls from p_0 to p_1, the consumers gain the area A, measured as $\Delta p Q$, and the excess of their willingness to pay for the additional output $(B + R)$ less what they actually pay (R), that is, the area B, measured as $\frac{1}{2}\Delta p \Delta Q$. While the project receives revenues R, measured as $p_1 \Delta Q$, other producers lose the area A on intramarginal production. This loss cancels out the intramarginal gains of the consumers, since the benefits and losses of different individuals are equally weighted. The net benefits are then $B + R$. This is expressed in domestic prices as

$$B_1 = B + R - (\text{SER})M - aN.$$

The expression in border prices is

$$B_2 = \beta B + rR - (\text{OER})M - bN,$$

where β is the consumption conversion factor. The two expressions, B_1 and B_2, are equivalent if $\beta = \alpha = \text{SCF}$ and $b = a(\text{SCF})$.

The use of the consumption conversion factor (β) may be explained as follows: Assume that the utility value of the area B is that represented by consumption expenditures of Rs100 at domestic prices. This amount corresponds to $\beta 100$ worth of expenditures in border prices, where β reflects the pattern of expenditures of the consumers, the prices they face, and the duties and taxes that bear on their purchases. If β is 0.8, then, by definition of β, Rs80 of expenditures in border prices produces the same utility as Rs100 of expenditures in domestic prices. Therefore, if the gain measured in domestic prices is B, its value when rescaled in terms of border prices is $\beta\ B$.[9]

Case 4. Consider the same case as in Case 3, but assume that the nontraded output is an intermediate product used by various industries. Assume further that these industries use the project output as an input in the production of a consumption good. For example, if the project output is fertilizer, then the output of those who use fertilizer is a consumption good, such as rice. The following discussion is simplified by this assumption, but the substance does not depend on it: one can just as well assume that the project's output is an input to an industry which, in turn, produces another input, and so on.

The analysis proceeds similarly. The intramarginal gains of users (A) are canceled by the intramarginal losses of other producers. However, the area B should now be interpreted differently. Let X be incremental sales of the output produced by the purchaser of the project's output, and let R and Y be its expenditures on the project's output and on other inputs, respectively.[10] Then the purchaser's profits corresponding to the incremental project production are $B = X - R - Y$; assume also that the prices of X and Y remain constant, since otherwise there will be additional surpluses to worry about. The expression in domestic prices is now

$$B_1 = B + R - (\text{SER})\,M - aN$$
$$= X - R - Y + R - (\text{SER})\,M - aN$$
$$= X - Y - (\text{SER})\,M - aN.$$

9. Or equivalently, one unit of border value must correspond to 1/0.8 or 1.25 units of domestic value. In a sense, therefore, the value of a unit of foreign exchange spent on consumption goods is 1.25 in terms of domestic values, and $1/\beta$ may be regarded as another interpretation of the shadow price of foreign exchange. Thus the actual exchange rate divided by the consumption conversion factor is another definition of the shadow exchange rate. In a sense this is the basic correspondence between the shadow exchange rate and the conversion factor approaches.

10. If the amounts of other inputs, which substitute for or complement the project output, do not change, the term Y is zero.

In border prices, this is written as:

$$B_2 = xX - yY - (\text{OER})M - bN,$$

where x and y are the conversion factors appropriate for converting X and Y, respectively, into border prices. The two expressions will be equivalent if $x = y = \text{SCF}$ and $b = a(\text{SCF})$.

Some common approximations

Given that average conversion factors must be used in project analysis, the question arises as to which kinds of aggregates are most useful in practice. The average factors most commonly used are briefly discussed below.

For supply-price conversion factors, it has been found useful to estimate averages for some of the major project cost categories, such as civil construction, transport, and electric power. Such general factors, based on a revaluation in border prices of the costs of such inputs, are, of course, to be used only when further disaggregations are not warranted. When additional detail is needed, further breakdowns have to be undertaken— for example, the transport conversion factor must be replaced by a conversion factor specific to the type of traffic, mode of transport, and distances involved.

Another general conversion factor concerns the cost of labor. Although there are many labor conversion factors—for each principal type of labor classified by skill, location, season, and so on—only a few types of labor are likely to be important in any project. Detailed work may not be warranted for the unimportant categories of labor, in which case a general conversion factor may be used.

Project costs usually include the costs of raw material and various equipment. When these costs are not a major part of total costs, a general factor suffices to convert them into border prices. Even when they are a major part, they may consist of many small components. A general factor may still be useful if the detailed work in calculating specific factors for each such component is too costly or infeasible. Thus, general factors are often estimated for such broad categories as raw material and intermediate goods.

All projects involve transport and distribution costs, which must also be revalued in border prices. It is usually easier to separate out the transport and distribution costs and convert them by an appropriately defined general factor for this category of cost, rather than to include such costs in defining individual or general conversion factors for the inputs and outputs concerned.

The most common practice, however, is not to use general factors for each of the main cost categories, but to use a standard conversion factor

(SCF)—or a general SER—which is much broader than any of the general factors mentioned above. The standard conversion factor is an economywide aggregate, averaged over all goods and services produced in the economy, most of which have no relevance to the project being evaluated.[11] Unless the SCF happens to be close to all the other factors for transport, power, construction, raw material, and so on, this practice will introduce significant errors. The transport conversion factor may, for example, be 1.5, indicating a large subsidy on transport perhaps because of subsidized domestic sales of fuel, whereas the SCF may be 0.8, showing that fuel subsidies are outweighed in the economy as a whole by taxes on other commodities.[12]

As general supply-price conversion factors are helpful for various categories of nontraded inputs, general demand-price conversion factors are helpful for various categories of nontraded outputs.

A general food-grain conversion factor, along the lines illustrated earlier in the sorghum-rice-maize example, is useful for evaluating nontraded agricultural outputs. General factors may also be estimated for such nontraded project outputs as transport and public utilities; they are derived from the conversion factors for the goods and services which substitute for or complement, say, electricity use. They should be distinguished from the general supply-price conversion factors, which relate to cost of producing, say, electricity. Confusion between supply-price and demand-price factors frequently lead to errors. Even more general factors may be estimated for evaluating nontraded project outputs belonging to such categories as raw material or intermediate goods. If, for example, an electricity demand-price conversion factor is not available, a general demand-price factor for intermediate goods may be used for evaluating the industrial component of electricity consumption.

The consumption conversion factor (CCF) mentioned earlier is one of the most important aggregates in general use. It is a weighted average of conversion factors for all goods entering into final consumption in the economy and may be used when more specific factors are not available. Since the consumption baskets for different income groups vary, the CCF will vary for each income group. For general purposes, the relevant consumer group is usually taken as that with the national average income.

---

11. The SCF, if it is to be used to convert supply prices, must be based on production weights. Imports of goods not produced at home should be excluded from the aggregate. This is the sense in which the SCF is defined in Little and Mirrlees (1974, p. 218).

12. The evidence from the countries in which many conversion factors have been estimated suggests considerable variations across sectors and commodities. In fact, SCF estimates are often close to unity, even in countries where wide disparities between domestic and border prices exist in major sectors. See, for example, Hughes (1980a, 1980b), Page (1982), Powers (1981), and Schohl (1979).

General conversion factors of a similar type may also be estimated for other broad categories of expenditures, such as investment. An economywide SCF may also be estimated for the purpose of demand-price conversions. In that case, the SCF should be calculated on the basis of demand weights—excluding exports which are, at the margin, not consumed or used at home. This is to be distinguished from the supply-price SCF referred to earlier. (In an exercise for Nigeria a few years ago, for example, Mustapha Rouis estimated the supply-price SCF as 0.83 and the demand-price SCF as 0.69.)

Estimation of averages

The most common method of estimating general factors is disaggregation of costs. Usually a few rounds of disaggregation, and then the use of an SCF, suffice to produce acceptable estimates of supply-price factors for nontraded goods.

Another common technique is to use trade data, which are among the most readily available data in developing countries.[13] For example, a simple proxy for the SCF would be the average duty

$$SCF = \frac{M + X}{M' + X'},$$

where M, X are, respectively, imports and exports in border prices, and M', X' are imports and exports in domestic market prices.[14] General conversion factors for consumption goods, capital goods, and so on can be readily calculated by using more detailed trade data—for example, the CCF can be derived for imports and exports of consumption goods alone. When this approach is used to estimate supply-price factors, all imports of goods not produced at home should be excluded; when it is used to estimate the demand-price factors (such as the CCF), all exports of goods not used at home should be excluded.

There are several problems with the above approach. First, it assumes that all imports and exports take place at constant border prices. Many countries, however, produce exports whose world market prices are affected by the volume of exports. The formula then has to be amended for such terms of trade effects. If, for example, the exports of a good, such as tea, would depress world market prices, the SCF should be lower than the one estimated by the above formula. The correct formula would then be

$$SCF = \frac{M + X_1 + X_2(1/1 - N)}{M' + X'},$$

---

13. See, for example, Bruce (1976), Linn (1977), and Squire, Little, and Durdag (1979).

14. This formula and the one in the following paragraph are derived in Appendix B to this chapter.

where X_2 is the exports of tea, X_1 represents all other exports, and N is the absolute value of the elasticity of world demand for tea faced by the country.

Second, this approach ignores nontraded goods. This is a major shortcoming, since to do so is justified only if nontraded goods are not an important element of the conversion factor being estimated, or if the conversion factor for the excluded nontraded goods equals the conversion factor being estimated.

Third, this approach is based on average shares in trade. Project expenditures on inputs, or revenues from sales of product output, however, represent marginal changes. Thus, the formula is strictly applicable only if average and marginal trade shares are equal. The formula can, of course, be amended to reflect differences between average and marginal shares.[15]

Fourth, this approach does not adequately deal with quotas or other types of quantitative restrictions prevailing in some developing countries. If a quota is fully effective for an imported commodity, the project will not increase imports of that commodity. Thus, the commodity will be ignored. If, however, the quota is not fully effective, its tariff equivalent must be used instead of the import duty that may be nominally (but not in fact) applicable.[16] These implicit tariffs can be estimated only from a direct comparison of border and domestic market prices, adjusted for transport and distribution costs. This task requires work on each commodity affected and implies that the estimation of general factors must be abandoned. Although the widespread use of quantitative restrictions by a country renders this trade-data approach unreliable, it can nonetheless be useful if the conversion factors estimated (with such restrictions ignored) are upper limits to their true values. This would be the case if the quantitative restrictions impinge mostly on the import side.

The trade-data approach is, at best, a good starting point for the analysis of general conversion factors. One should look for other approaches that overcome one or more of the problems discussed above. For example, in estimating the CCF, it is preferable to use expenditure weights obtained from household expenditure surveys whenever possible, rather than the formula based on trade data alone.[17]

Both the cost-decomposition method and the trade-data approach tend to treat separate conversion factors as being mutually independent. If, however, a large subsidy on petroleum products is removed, or if there is a major reform of agricultural prices, a large number of conversion factors will be simultaneously affected. Taking account of such changes in only

15. See Linn (1977), pp. 15–17.

16. The treatment in this case depends on how the quantitative restriction is operated. See Appendix B for a particular case.

17. For an example of the estimation of the CCF along these lines, see Annex III of Squire, Little, and Durdag (1979).

some of the general factors may introduce serious errors. One way of proceeding in such cases is to use semi-input-output models. Following the extensive work of Scott, Hughes, and others on conversion factors, several useful experiments with such models have been made recently.[18]

In this approach, one starts by distinguishing between goods and services and a set of "primary" inputs—"primary" in the sense that their conversion factors are exogenously specified to begin with. The market prices of the various goods and services are then decomposed into primary inputs and other goods and services. For any good i, one can write

$$B_i = \sum_j \alpha_{ij} B_j + \sum_k \beta_{ik} W_k,$$

where $B_i, \ldots, B_j$ are border values of the goods and services involved, and W_k are the values of the relevant primary factors, also in border prices. Alternatively,

$$\frac{B_i}{M_i} = \sum_i \alpha_{ij} \frac{M_j}{M_i} \frac{B_j}{M_j} + \sum_k \beta_{ik} \frac{M_k}{M_i} \frac{W_k}{M_k},$$

where $M_i, i = 1, \ldots, j$, refer to market costs of goods and services, and M_k to the market costs of the primary factors.
Defining

$$\frac{B_i}{M_i} \equiv v_i; \quad \frac{W_k}{M_k} \equiv w_k$$

$$\alpha_{ij} \frac{M_j}{M_i} \equiv a_{ij}; \quad \beta_{ik} \frac{M_k}{M_i} \equiv b_{ik},$$

the expression becomes

$$v_i = \sum_j a_{ij} v_j + \sum_k b_{ik} w_k,$$

or, in matrix notation,

$$v = Av + Bw.$$

One can then solve for v as

$$v = [I - A]^{-1} Bw.$$

Since some of the primary input conversion factors will depend on the commodity conversion factors, an iterative procedure must be used to estimate w and v. Only a few iterations are needed.

---

18. See Scott, MacArthur, and Newbery (1974), Hughes (1980a, 1980b, 1983), Page (1982), Powers (1981), and Schohl (1979).

This approach has obvious advantages—it allows consistency checks, it enables one to trace out changes in tax and subsidy policies, and it facilitates updating. But it is not trouble free. For example, it is not easy for project analysts to understand the precise commodity or primary input classifications used; but this understanding is required to establish the correspondence between their data and the conversion factors resulting from the exercise.

It is more useful to build up estimates of conversion factors from detailed examinations of particular sectors rather than simply to use the material in existing input-output tables. By focusing attention on specific goods and services, the analyst can examine the effects of quotas and other trade restrictions, of government controls of domestic prices, of economies of scale and capacity underutilization, and of supply and demand elasticities for traded goods. The limitations of this disaggregative approach are those of time and data rather than of the analytical framework itself. Apart from yielding a large number of conversion factors, such detailed studies can also be very useful complements to studies of effective protection rates.

Adjustments to External Imbalance

Shadow prices often have to be estimated in periods of rapid economic adjustment that involve changes in trade barriers, exchange rates, and public deficits. Consider the standard representation of an economy in a disequilibrium situation shown in Figure 4. The figure shows three schedules: NN representing equilibrium in the home goods market, BB representing external balance, and YY showing output and income. The real exchange rate (e) is on the vertical axis: this is the ratio of P_T, the "composite" price of traded goods, to P_N, the "composite" price of nontraded goods. Absorption (E), consisting of home demand for traded and nontraded goods, and income (Y) are on the horizontal axis. Both E and Y are measured in terms of nontraded goods (for full details, see Dornbusch, 1980, pp 100–03).

The economy might be at a point like A_1, at which the home goods market is in equilibrium, but absorption exceeds income, the trade deficit being ($E_1 - Y_1$). There will be no need to change the nominal exchange rate if all domestic prices and wages are fully flexible downward, since reduced absorption in such a case will reduce P_N, thereby increasing the real exchange rate to its equilibrium value (e_0). With rigidity in P_N, one must devalue and simultaneously reduce absorption to restore equilibrium. Alternatively, the economy might be at a point like A_2, in which case the excess demand in the home goods market would produce domestic inflation. In either case, A_1 or A_2, the real exchange rate must be depreciated, inducing resource switches away from the nontraded sectors to

Figure 4. *Overall Equilibrium*

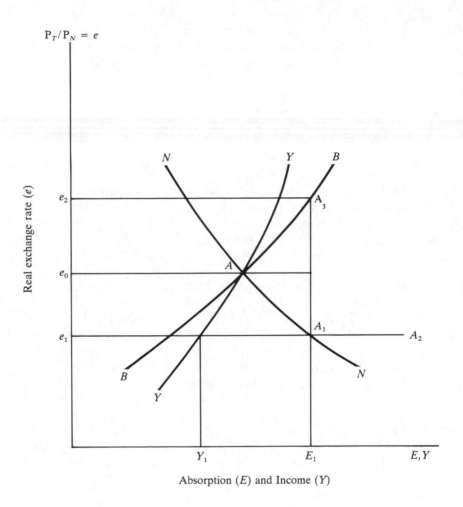

Absorption (E) and Income (Y)

Source: Dornbusch (1980), p. 101.

traded sectors. Lower real wages will induce increases in labor-intensive import substitution and in labor-intensive exports.

While this is too simple a characterization of the problems that developing countries have faced in recent years, it suggests that the approach to shadow pricing would in practice depend very much on the speed of adjustment and on whether the postadjustment shadow prices are likely to be significantly different from those relevant to the past experience. If it can be presumed that the crisis-ridden economy will soon return to the pre-crisis situation, it would perhaps be reasonable to ignore the transitory problems in estimating shadow prices and conversion factors. No significant biases are likely to be introduced by doing so except in the case of very short-lived projects.

The adjustment period may, however, be long enough to matter; the postadjustment economy may also be structurally different from the pre-crisis one. Conversion factors may change substantially and frequently, not only because of inflexibility in some domestic prices and wages, but also because of changes in public policies. Control of the public deficit will require changes in taxes. Moreover, governments frequently respond to external deficits by tightening and broadening the import quota regime. A characteristic of quota regimes is that the tariff equivalences of quotas can fluctuate, and such fluctuations cannot be ascertained except through the laborious process of direct comparisons between domestic and foreign prices.

The use of the foreign exchange numeraire in cost-benefit analysis has a great advantage in such situations, at least for foreign agencies which tend to prefer financing projects with large traded components. Typically export-oriented projects are preferred, even though efficient import substitution projects can be just as attractive in situations of external imbalance.

It is obvious that if project benefits stem from exports (X), and if imported inputs (M) dominate costs, then the net traded component $(X - M)$ will dominate other components. It is not necessary to determine domestic-foreign price disparities for this traded component since one can use foreign prices directly, at the actual exchange rates. Forecasting the evolution of the relevant foreign prices may not be easy, but this problem is the same regardless of whether the developing country is or is not in a crisis. Few such countries have the market power to influence the foreign prices of its imports and exports; even when such power exists (as in, say, Brazil), it is likely to be restricted to a few commodities.

Moreover, the traded component need not be confined to direct exports and imports. As discussed previously, local costs can be disaggregated into traded and nontraded components. Taking both directly and indirectly traded components, the overall influence of foreign prices can be increased in project analysis, thereby reducing the importance of any errors that one might make in treating nontraded elements. It will be preferable to avoid the use of domestic market prices as much as possible.

To illustrate, suppose the net benefits of a project, in border prices, is

$$B = rR - bL,$$

where r is a demand-price conversion factor for the incremental revenues, R, generated by a nontraded project output, and b is the conversion factor for labor, L, which is assumed to be the only project input.

As far as the revenues are concerned, let

$$rR = \sum_i r_i R_i,$$

where r_i and R_i are, respectively, the conversion factors and expenditures on other products. The expenditures on project output, as discussed earlier, is the net effect of reallocations of expenditures on related products. With p_i and Q_i being, respectively, the prices and quantities of the other products, one can also write

$$rR = \sum_i r_i p_i Q_i.$$

Now if some of the related products are traded, say, products j to n, then their border prices, b_i, can be used directly. That is,

$$rR = \sum_i^{j-1} r_i p_i Q_i + \sum_j^n b_i Q_i.$$

The amount of precision can be increased by further disaggregating the i to $j-1$ elements.

The treatment of the labor element can proceed exactly similarly. Instead of using the market wage as a measure of labor's marginal productivity, the effects on different labor markets can be evaluated directly in terms of foreign prices—relatively easily when labor is withdrawn from sectors producing traded goods.

This procedure is exactly the same as the one discussed earlier, except that it is more direct and reduces the importance of using conversion factors. It might be worthwhile going into greater accounting details when the relative prices of nontraded items (and therefore conversion factors) are likely to change significantly. It is not my intention, however, to suggest that all problems in evaluation can be avoided by this procedure in periods of economic stabilization. To begin with, the extent of disaggregation necessary to reach the desired degree of precision may simply be infeasible. At least two other problems deserve some comment.

Labor

It was suggested above that at least that part of the project labor that is withdrawn from the traded goods sector can be border-priced directly; the rest of the labor can be similarly treated if the cost of doing so is worth the precision gained. This, however, is not as easy as it sounds, even in principle, since the marginal physical product of labor should change during the stabilization period. Reallocation of labor to the traded goods sector will lower its marginal physical productivity in that sector. Economic stabilization, as indicated earlier, is likely to require a decline in the real wage rate. An estimate of this decline must be made in order to value labor.

The change in the real wage rate required to respond to an external imbalance need not, however, be always large. At any rate, there is often a tendency to overestimate the required change—for two reasons. First, the extent of the real depreciation of the exchange rate needed is sometimes grossly overestimated by focusing only on the balance of payments equation. At a point like A_1 in Figure 4, the required adjustment in the real exchange rate is $(e_0 - e_1)$; this may be much less than we will get if we focus only on the BB curve (that is, $e_2 - e_1$). Second, the required change in the real wage rate will depend on how large employment is in the nontraded goods sector relative to the traded goods sector. Assuming that the elasticities of labor demand are equal in the two sectors, and employment is evenly divided, the required change will be half the required change in the real exchange rate.

To illustrate, assume a competitive economy with a common equilibrium wage, W, in nominal terms. Assume also that shadow and market prices are equal. Then labor market equilibrium requires

$$W = P_T \alpha = P_N \beta,$$

where α and β are the marginal physical products in traded and nontraded sectors. The real wage (q), in terms of traded goods, is

$$q \equiv W/P_T = \alpha = \beta/e, \quad \text{with} \quad e \equiv P_T/P_N.$$

If P_T is constant, then the nominal wage, W, and α will fall in the same proportion as we move from A_1 to A (Figure 4). Prices of nontraded goods, however, will fall more than W, and β will rise. The proportional change in the shadow wage rate (SWR) will simply be, allowing for foreign inflation,

$$d \log \text{SWR}/dt = d \log P_T/dt + d \log \alpha/dt.$$

Moreover, it can be shown that

$$d \log \text{SWR}/dt = d \log P_T/dt - x dt$$

where x is the fraction of labor employed in the nontraded sector (assuming equal elasticities of demand in the two sectors).

Public budget

The discussion thus far suggests that the net benefits of a project that involves only traded elements would not be affected by a transitory period of economic stabilization. Thus, if two projects yield an annual stream of net benefits, $X - M$, and are evaluated at the same predicted actual exchange rates, then their present worth will be identical.

This conclusion may be wrong if the profits of the two projects are distributed differently. For example, if public income becomes more valuable at the margin than private sector income during the period of economic stabilization, then the project which yields more benefits to the public sector will be preferred. Similarly, if investments, private or public, become more valuable at the margin than consumption, then again the relative merits of the two projects will depend on their impact on investments and consumption.

Some authors, such as Little amd Mirrlees (1974), have suggested that major changes in the shadow wage rate in response to external imbalance will occur primarily through the change in the consumption cost of employing industrial labor. For this to be true, one must have a real wage gap between the industrial and agricultural sectors ($c - m$ in their notation). This gap will increase if the industrial real wage (in border prices, c) is fixed and if the marginal product of labor in agriculture in border prices (m) falls following a devaluation. The increase in the wage gap will, however, increase the shadow wage rate in their approach, other things being equal. If the shadow wage rate is to fall, the shadow price of investments must increase sufficiently to more than offset the increase in the wage gap. In fact, Little and Mirrlees assume no change in m. The shadow price of investments need then increase by less to make devaluations effective.

The discount rate to be used may also change. It is commonly thought that the public sector should prefer projects with shorter gestation periods in times of crisis because of the greater scarcity of budgetary resources. However, if the discount rate is defined in terms of the consumption numeraire, then changes in that rate, if any, will be small. The discount rate may even fall. If scarcity of budgetary resources is the main issue, a premium on such resources should then be introduced—along the lines of Dasgupta, Marglin, and Sen (1972) and Little and Mirrlees (1974). If the discount rate is instead defined in terms of the public income numeraire, then it may temporarily increase during the stabilization period. These types of concepts are discussed in the next chapter.

Appendix A. The Domestic Resource Cost Method

The domestic resource cost (DRC) method is widely used in resource allocation studies, especially those which focus on entire sectors or large parts of the economy. The DRC concept, like all popular concepts, has several variants which are reviewed, from a theoretical point of view, by Srinivasan and Bhagwati (1978). The purpose here is to bring out its relationship to the conversion factor approach in very simple terms.

Let the net benefits of a project, lasting only one year, be (in border values)

$$B = \sum_i (E_i - M_i) - \sum_j c_j N_j,$$

where E_i, M_i are exported and imported outputs and inputs, c_j are conversion factors, and N_j are nontraded inputs.

The criterion $B \geq 0$ implies

$$\frac{\sum_j c_j N_j}{\sum_i (E_i - M_i)} \leq 1.$$

This is a pure foreign exchange ratio, since both the numerator and the denominator are measured in terms of foreign exchange. Domestic resource costs are not distinguishable from foreign exchange costs and benefits in the conversion factor approach.

Suppose, however, an economywide conversion factor, c, has been estimated. Defining $c_j \equiv c\gamma_j$, one can rewrite the criterion as

$$\frac{cK}{F} \leq 1,$$

where $K \equiv \sum \gamma_i N_j$, and $F \equiv \sum (E_i - M_i)$. Define $F' \equiv F/\text{OER}$ as the value of $\sum(E_i - M_i)$ in terms of foreign currencies, and $s \equiv \text{OER}/c$ as a shadow exchange rate corresponding to the economywide conversion factor. Thus, one can alternatively write $K/F' \leq s$. The term K/F' may be interpreted as the domestic resource costs of nontraded inputs (in terms of adjusted market prices) needed to produce a unit of foreign exchange. Thus, the project is acceptable if this ratio is less than or equal to the economywide shadow exchange rate. This interpretation is even more straightforward if $c = c_j$ so that $\gamma_j = 1$.

Another way of expressing the same criterion would be to divide throughout by s, in which case $K' \equiv K/s$ is the dollar value of domestic costs. In that case $D \equiv K'/F' < 1$, and D is a DRC coefficient.

The DRC method can, therefore, be defined in a way that is equivalent to the conversion factor approach. There are, however, two difficulties with the method.

First, the DRC measure is prone to classification errors. Suppose, for example, that transport costs, N_t, can be subdivided into a traded component, N_{t1}, and a nontraded component (say, labor), N_{t2}. The conversion factor for transport is c_t, consisting of adjustments to both N_{t1} and N_{t2}, that is,

$$c_t N_t = c_{t1} N_{t1} + c_{t2} N_{t2}.$$

Dividing throughout by the general factor c, this becomes

$$\gamma_t N_t = \gamma_{t1} N_{t1} + \gamma_{t2} N_{t2}.$$

Since the component N_{t1} should be transferred to the denominator, $\gamma_t N_t$ can no longer be interpreted as domestic resource costs. This problem may arise also in the case of labor costs (N_{t2}) since, in the presence of full employment, the shadow wage rate is simply the output forgone at the margin, which directly or indirectly will represent foreign exchange sacrificed. The line between domestic and foreign costs is quite ambiguous, making it difficult to compare the analysis of a project with those of other projects, or to judge comparative advantage at the sectoral level.

Second, the DRC measure is in the form of a ratio and, as such, it has the same problem that cost-benefit ratios generally do in the context of investment criteria. It cannot be used to compare mutually exclusive project options, which is a central part of project analysis. The option with the highest net present value is not necessarily the one with the best DRC ratio. If benefits are 2 and costs are 1, the cost-benefit ratio is 0.5 and the net present value is 1. If benefits are 20 and costs are 11, the ratio is 0.55 and the net present value is 9. The better project can thus have a higher cost-benefit ratio.

Appendix B. Some Formulas for Conversion Factors

The general definition of a conversion factor is: let a marginal change in expenditures on a commodity i be V_i when measured in domestic market prices, and W_i when measured in border prices (adjusted as necessary to reflect changes in border prices). Then the conversion factor for the commodity i is

$$c_i = dW_i/dV_i \tag{4.1a}$$

For any arbitrary collection of goods, $i = 1, \ldots, K$, a marginal change in expenditures involving these goods may be written as

$$dV \equiv \sum_{i=1}^{K} dV_i.$$

The conversion factor for this unit of expenditure is

$$c \equiv dW/dV \equiv \sum_i c_i m_i, \tag{4.1b}$$

where $m_i \equiv V_i/V$ is the marginal share of good i.

In the next section, the conversion factors appropriate for individual commodities, as in equation (4.1a), will be discussed. The adjustments necessary for tariffs, quotas, transport costs, and trade inelasticities will be pointed out. The last two sections discuss special cases of aggregate or general conversion factors, as in equation (4.1b).

Commodity conversion factors

A commodity will be either imported, exported, or not traded. The conversion factor for an importable is discussed first.

Let s denote the share of domestic production in total domestic use or consumption; $(1 - s)$ is thus the share of imports. Let $N(d)$ be the price elasticity of home demand (positive value), $E(d)$ the price elasticity of home supply, and $E(w)$ the price elasticity of world supply relevant to the country concerned. Ignoring distributional effects, the conversion factor for the commodity may then be written as

$$C_m = \frac{s\alpha E(d) + \beta N(d) + (1 - s)[1 + E(w)]}{sE(d) + (1 - s)E(w) + N(d)},$$

where α, β are conversion factors applicable to the supply price and the demand price, respectively. Usually it is assumed that the imports of a developing country do not affect world prices. In this case, $E(w) \to \infty$ and $C_m = 1$. If, at the margin, incremental demand is met entirely from imports, $N(d) = 0$ or $s = 0$, then $C_m = 1 + 1/E(w)$.

But the formula above assumes that domestic prices and border prices are equal, that is, there are no tariffs, taxes, or transport costs. The differential between the border and domestic prices may be proportional (ad valorem) or fixed. Usually tariffs, sales taxes, and at least a part of transport (and distribution) costs are ad valorem. For an ad valorem differential, t, the formula becomes

$$C_m = \frac{s\alpha E(d) + \beta N(d) + (1 - s)(1 + E)^{-1}[1 + E(w)]}{sE(d) + (1 - s)E(w) + N(d)}. \tag{4.2a}$$

This formula, however, which is in terms of domestic supply elasticity, $E(d)$, and the domestic demand elasticity, $N(d)$, may be expressed also in terms of the elasticity of demand for imports, $M(d)$. Since

$$M(d) \equiv \frac{1}{1 - s} N(d) + \frac{s}{1 - s} E(d).$$

or

$$N(d) + sE(d) = (1 - s)M(d),$$

the market value of the change in expenditure is

$$dV = (1 - s)[M(d) + E(w)].$$

Moreover, if the conversion factors β and α in equation (4.2a) above are approximately equal, then

$$\beta N(d) + s\alpha E(d) = \beta(1 - s)M(d),$$

and the value in border prices, dW, is

$$(1 - s)[\beta M(d) + E(w) + 1].$$

Hence, the conversion factor is

$$C_m = \frac{\beta M(d) + E(w) + 1}{M(d) + E(w)}.$$

Note that only "trade" elasticities appear in this formula. Furthermore, if there is a tariff (or ad valorem differential), t, this becomes

$$C_m = \frac{\beta M(d) + (1 + t)^{-1}[1 + E(w)]}{M(d) + E(w)}. \tag{4.2b}$$

The important special cases are (1) constant border price $e(W) \to \infty$,

$$C_m = (1 + t)^{-1} \tag{4.2c}$$

and (2) specialization (incremental project demand being met from imports only), that is, $M(d) = N(d) = E(d) = 0$,

$$C_m = (1 + t)^{-1}\left[1 + \frac{1}{E(w)}\right]. \tag{4.2d}$$

For an exportable good,

$N(d) =$ positive value of the price elasticity of domestic demand
$N(w) =$ positive value of the price elasticity of world demand
$E(d) =$ price elasticity of domestic supply
$\quad a =$ share of domestic demand in total production
$\quad t =$ export tax or ad valorem differential between domestic and export prices, such that (domestic price) $= (1 - t)$ (FOB price).

Then the conversion factor for an exportable is

$$C_x = \frac{\alpha E(d) - (1 - a)(1 - t)^{-1}[1 - N(w)] + a\beta N(d)}{E(d) + (1 - a)N(w) + aN(d)}.$$

Equivalently, this can be written in terms of the elasticity of export supply, $X(d)$, and of export demand, $N(w)$, as (assuming $\alpha = \beta$),

$$C_x = \frac{\alpha X(d) - (1 - t)^{-1}[1 - N(w)]}{X(d) + N(w)}. \tag{4.2e}$$

The important special cases are (1) constant border price $N(w) \to \infty$,

$$C_x = (1 - t)^{-1} \tag{4.2f}$$

and (2) specialization (incremental demand is met at the expense of exports only), that is, $X(d) = 0$,

$$C_x = (1 - t)^{-1}\left[1 - \frac{1}{N(w)}\right]. \tag{4.2g}$$

For a nontradable good, the conversion factor involves only domestic price elasticities:

$$C_n = \frac{\alpha E(d) + \beta N(d)}{E(d) + N(d)} \qquad (4.2h)$$

with $E(d) =$ price elasticity of domestic supply
$N(d) =$ price elasticity of domestic demand (positive value)
$\alpha, \beta =$ conversion factors relevant to the supply price and the demand price, respectively.

If unit costs are constant, $E(d) \rightarrow \infty$,

$$C_n = \alpha.$$

If supply is inelastic, $E(d) = 0$,

$$C_n = \beta.$$

If demand is perfectly elastic, $N(d) \rightarrow \infty$,

$$C_n = \beta.$$

Goods and services which are tradable, but are not traded at the margin because of quantitative restrictions, should be treated as nontraded goods. A mixed case would be when a quota is partially lifted at the time of the project, so that the good concerned is partially obtained from abroad and partially from home production. The imported part should then be valued at the border price, assuming this is constant, and the locally produced part should be valued as a nontraded good.

Finally, transport costs which depend on the volume transported rather than on the value of the product can be taken care of simply. One would apply a conversion factor, calculated as discussed so far, on the expenditures on the product net of volume-related transport costs, and add these to the transport costs converted to border prices separately. Thus, if dV_1 is expenditures on the product net of transport costs with c_1 the appropriate conversion factor, and if transport costs are dV_2 with c_2 as the conversion factor, the overall conversion factor for the product would be

$$c\,dV = c_1\,dV_1 + c_2\,dV_2,$$

where $$dV = dV_1 + dV_2.$$

General conversion factors

Various types of aggregate or general conversion factors can be defined on the basis of the commodity conversion factors and the marginal shares of the various commodities. The most common aggregates are the standard conversion factor, which is an all-purpose conversion factor, and the consumption conversion factor. The differences between different aggregates result from the differences in the weights of various commodities. Some special cases are discussed below.

Optimal policies. If there are no distortions in the economy, all conversion factors will be unity. Domestic market values will equal border prices, allowing only for transport costs and optimal trade taxes and subsidies. To illustrate, in the formula (4.2h) for nontradables, $\alpha = \beta = 1$, therefore $Cn = 1$. Similarly, consider the formula for the importable (4.2b): set $\beta = 1$ and let the import tariff be $1/E(w)$, this being the value of the optimum tariff; the conversion factor then becomes unity. The conversion factor for an exportable—equation (4.2e) above—would also be unity if the export tax is optimal, that is, if it equals $1/N(w)$.

No nontradables. Nontradables can be ignored if their share is very small or if their conversion factors equal the one being calculated. In that case, the general conversion factors become much simpler. If border prices are constant, the change in expenditures in domestic prices (dV) will equal the value of imports (dM) and exports (dX) adjusted for import and export taxes. That is,

$$dV = \sum_i (1 + t_m)dM_i + \sum_j (1 - t_x)dX_j,$$

and the conversion factor would be

$$c = dW/dV = \left(\sum dM_i + \sum dX_j \right) \bigg/ dV.$$

But if it is further assumed that marginal and average shares are equal, that is,

$$dM_i/dV = M_i/V, \quad dX_j/dV = X_j/V,$$

then
$$c = \frac{M + X}{(1 + t_m)M + (1 - t_x)X}, \tag{4.3a}$$

where M and X are total values of imports and exports in border prices, and the denominator is their values in domestic prices. If it is judged that exportables have a low weight, this formula can be written simply as the inverse of the generalized tariff rate, that is,

$$c = \frac{M}{(1 + t_m)M} = \frac{1}{1 + t_m}. \tag{4.3b}$$

Frequently a more appropriate formulation would be to allow for the variability of some export prices. If dX_1 is the expenditure on an export product facing an inelastic foreign demand, and t_x is the duty on exports, and $dX_1 + dX_2 = dX$, then the change in domestic expenditure can be written as

$$dV = (1 + t_m)dM + (1 - t_x)dX.$$

If the marginal and average shares in trade are equal, the corresponding conversion factor would be

$$c = \frac{M + X_2 + c_1(1 - t_x)X_1}{(1 + t_m)M + (1 - t_x)X},$$ (4.3c)

with c_1 the conversion factor for an export product. For example, if c_1 is as defined in equation (4.2g), then

$$c_1(1 - t_x) = \left(1 - \frac{1}{N(w)}\right).$$

Usually this would be less than unity, and thus the effect of inelastic export demand would be to reduce the value of the conversion factor.

CHAPTER 5

Consumption, Investment, and Interest Rates

THE WEIGHTING OF INCOME or consumption changes occurring at a point in time was discussed in Chapters 2 and 3. Intertemporal weighting raises similar issues, on which there is a vast literature. Only the main aspects are reviewed in this chapter.

If the purpose of analysis is to compare consumption changes over time, then the basic discount rate should clearly reflect the rate of decline in the welfare value of consumption over time. Such a discount rate is usually called the consumption rate of interest (CRI). A social valuation function must be used to define what is meant by consumption gains and losses and how they are to be compared. It is obvious that the types of issues involved are similar to those discussed in Chapters 2 and 3.

One possibility is to refer to how an individual would weight his or her consumption changes over time, that is, to his or her private rate of interest (PRI). A problem with this approach is that the PRI's of different persons may well differ. This may be because not all persons participate in capital market transactions. Even if they do, the incidence of income taxes at the margin may differ. If the market does not, for these reasons, equalize the PRI's, multiple discount rates may have to be used in cost-benefit analysis, and this may be an impractical proposition. There is still another problem. The consumption changes brought about by a project typically accrue to different generations, so that intergenerational welfare comparisons need to be made.

The next three sections deal with these questions. The definition of the CRI commonly used in the literature is presented in the first section, following which some implications of multiple discount rates and the appropriateness of using the market interest rate in cost-benefit analysis are discussed.

The rate of return to investments at the margin must also, of course, be introduced in the analysis. There are several different investment rates of interest (IRI) that can be considered. Even if the IRI is defined in efficiency prices, as assumed henceforth, it can differ between different sectors in the economy. For example, the IRI for the public sector is commonly believed to be lower than the IRI for the private sector in most countries. Also, the IRI for the private sector typically differs significantly from the private rate of return, if only because of business taxes; the IRI also differs in different parts of the private sector. It is frequently thought, nonetheless, that an efficiency rate of return for the economy as a whole—that is, a weighted average of IRI's (sometimes called the marginal productivity of capital)—is the appropriate discount rate for cost-benefit analysis. There is no reason, however, to presume that such an IRI for the economy will equal the CRI, however defined. Even if the capital market functions well, and even if there is a common PRI, the existence of various kinds of taxes will tend to drive a wedge between the IRI and the PRI. Defining CRI as the PRI will not therefore necessarily resolve the problem.

The possible inequality between IRI and CRI calls for special adjustments in cost-benefit analysis. The need for adjustments is not the issue; rather, it is the type of adjustment required. There are essentially two competing methods: one uses a shadow price for investments and the other uses an average of IRI and CRI. These two methods are discussed in this chapter in some detail, especially the variant owing to Little and Mirrlees.

The Social Rate of Interest

The consumption rate of interest (CRI) is the rate at which the value of consumption, in terms of a social welfare function W, falls over time. One element of this rate of fall might be a pure time discount factor. Regardless of what happens to consumption levels, there might be a case for discounting future consumption. The case might indeed be strong if society is expected to have a short life. More generally, the use of a time discount may be interpreted as reflecting the probability of extinction (see Dasgupta and Heal, 1979, p. 263). If this probability is negligible, however, the case for pure time discounting becomes highly questionable.

Let us ignore intratemporal issues, and assume a set of consumers with identical utility functions and consumption levels. The welfare function is defined as

$$W = W(\{U(C_t)\}),$$

where $U(C_t)$ is the utility level in period t.

The effect on social welfare of a stream of changes in consumption benefits brought about by a project, namely $\{dC_t\}$, can then be expressed as

$$dW = \sum_{t=0} \gamma_t dU_t,$$

where $\gamma_t \equiv \partial W/\partial U_t$ is the utility weight in period t, and dW is of course the net present value of the project in utility units. If this is normalized with respect to the current year, the net worth is

$$dU(C_0) + \sum_{t=1} \frac{\gamma_t}{\gamma_0} dU(C_t).$$

The pure rate of social time preference, or the utility discount rate, ρ_t, between any two periods is now simply

$$\rho_t = \frac{\gamma_t - \gamma_{t+1}}{\gamma_{t+1}} \geq 0,$$

assuming $\gamma_t \geq \gamma_{t+1}$ (gains in year t are at least as valuable as gains in year $t + 1$). This yields

$$\frac{\gamma_{t+1}}{\gamma_t} = \frac{1}{1 + \rho_t}.$$

If ρ is constant over time, we get the familiar net worth expression

$$dW = \sum_{t=0}^{\infty} \frac{1}{(1 + \rho)^t} dU(C_t).$$

Since there is a plausible case for regarding $\rho = 0$, discounting may not be appropriate at all if pure time preference were the only consideration.

There is, however, another consideration. The CRI relates W to consumption levels, not to utility levels. We are interested in the rate of fall of $[\gamma_t U_t']$, not just in the rate of fall of γ_t. Taking the effect of consumption changes on utility levels, the CRI is defined as

$$CRI_t = \eta_t g_t + \rho_t,$$

or, with constant parameters,

$$CRI = \eta g + \rho,$$

with η as the elasticity of marginal welfare of consumption and g as the expected rate of growth of consumption. If the marginal value of consumption is highly sensitive to what happens to consumption levels (η is high), or if consumption grows fast (g is high), the CRI can be a high positive number even if $\rho = 0$ (see Dasgupta and Heal, 1979, pp. 284–86 and 293, and Squire and van der Tak, 1975, pp. 139–40).

Some readers may wonder about the symmetry of this discussion with that in Chapter 3, where the subscript i was used to refer to the U and C of different persons in a given period. Since there was no weighting independent of consumption levels, the parameter γ did not appear. However, if we write t instead of i, substitute equation (3.4) into equation (3.1), and assume $\alpha = 1$, then we can readily derive $CRI = \eta g$, where $\eta = m(1 - \varepsilon) + \varepsilon = \varepsilon$, since $m = 0$. The parameter γ can also, of course, be introduced in equation (3.1) to derive the full definition of the CRI given in the previous paragraph. The CRI formula will become more complex if W is not utilitarian ($\alpha > 1$).

An individual's private consumption rate of interest (PRI) can be expressed in an analogous manner. In that case the pure rate of time preference cannot be readily ignored. Time discounting may be justified from an individual point of view even when it is not justified from the social point of view.

Multiple Discount Rates

One may prefer to choose the PRI as the social rate of interest. But the private interest rates, as mentioned earlier, may well differ across individuals. In that case, one will have to discount the gains and losses of an individual at his or her own discount rate. Calculating an average PRI cannot work, since the weights used in that average will, in general, differ from one period to the next—the distribution of the gains and losses owing to a project need not remain constant over time. Thus, Group A, with a PRI of 5 percent, may bear the costs, and Group B, with a PRI of 8 percent, may reap the benefits. Any theory that assumes the validity of an average PRI must be suspect unless one has reason to believe that the PRI's are very close to each other or that there is a mechanism to ensure that the distribution of all costs and benefits is the same for all periods and across all projects.

This problem also arises when the social rate of interest is determined differently. Thus, suppose that $\rho = 0$. The CRI for Group A would then be $\eta_a g_a$, and that for B, $\eta_b g_b$. If one assumes that $\eta_a = \eta_b$, or if one uses a single η exogenously, there is still the likelihood that the expected rates of growth of consumption of different groups will differ.

Consider two individuals (or groups) with different initial consumption levels and with different expected growth rates. First, assume A's initial consumption level (C_a^0) remains constant, while that of B (C_b^0) grows at rate g over time. Assume also $C_b^0 = \theta C_a^0$. Then defining

$$W \equiv U_a + U_b,$$

and using the constant-elasticity form, the weight on B's consumption compared with that of A's is

$$d_t \equiv \frac{U'(C_b^t)}{U'(C_a^0)}$$

$$= (C_b^t)^{-\eta} / (C_a^0)^{-\eta}$$

$$= [\theta C_a^0 e^{gt}]^{-\eta} / (C_a^0)^{-\eta}$$

$$= \theta^{-\eta} e^{-\eta g t}.$$

More generally, if C_a grows at g_a, and if C_b grows at g_b,

$$d_t = \theta^{-\eta} \frac{e^{-\eta g_a t}}{e^{-\eta g_b t}}.$$

The CRI appropriate for B differs from that appropriate for A, but this is taken account of in the time path of d_t. If A becomes progressively richer than B, the relative weight applicable for B increases over time.

One can therefore use either different discount rates for different individuals or changing relative weights over time. To illustrate numerically, suppose that A's consumption level is 100 units in period I and 110 units in period II, while B's consumption level is 50 in period I and 51 in period II. Suppose also that $\eta = 1$, so that B's consumption is twice as valuable as A's in the initial period (this weighting should be applied only for marginal changes, but this technical problem is ignored here for simplicity). One can now calculate the present value of total consumption in two equivalent ways:

$$\text{Method I} : \left(100 + \frac{110}{1.10}\right) + \left[2(50) + \frac{2(51)}{1.02}\right] = 400$$

$$\text{Method II}: \left(100 + \frac{110}{1.10}\right) + \left[2(50) + \frac{51(110/51)}{1.10}\right] = 400.$$

Method I used different discount rates, and Method II a different distribution weight for period II (namely, approximately 2.2). The important point is that differential distribution weights must be introduced if a single discount rate is used when a multiplicity of such rates is appropriate. This conclusion remains true if one assumes nonconstant and different elasticities for different individuals.

In a situation in which different groups of consumers are expected to experience different rates of growth of consumption, one must therefore select a group to which the CRI can be related. Some authors, following Squire and van der Tak (1975), define the CRI as $\eta \, \bar{g} + \rho$, where $\bar{g}$ is the expected rate of growth of per capita consumption in the country—as far as indicators go this may be the easiest one to measure. The distribution weights are correspondingly scaled to that level; that is, the weight on marginal consumption of someone at the per capital level is unity. As discussed in Chapter 3, the weight d_i for group i is then $d_{it} \equiv (\bar{C}_t/C_{it})^{\eta}$, where $\bar{C}_t$ is the per capita level. Alternatively, one may choose the critical consumption level (CCL) as the reference point, in which case

$$d_{it} = (\text{CCL}_t/C_{it})^{\eta}.$$

The CCL, to be discussed subsequently, is the level of consumption at which marginal gains in consumption are as valuable as marginal gains in public income.[1]

---

1. This reference point is used by such authors as Scott, MacArthur, and Newbery (1974) and Lal (1980).

The Appropriateness of the Market Interest Rate

It is perhaps heroic to assume that the market interest rate in developing countries reflects a unique private consumption interest rate. Even if it does, the appropriateness of the market interest rate may be challenged on many grounds. For example, Dasgupta, Marglin, and Sen (1972) suggest, among other things, that it is implausible to assume that individuals can optimize rationally over time. The learning process available to individuals in optimizing current purchases is not available in decisions over time, since one cannot revise past decisions.

The possibility that private rates of time preference might be higher than the social one was mentioned earlier. This possibility has been much discussed in the literature following the works of Sen (1967) and Marglin (1963). The argument is simply that each member of the present generation may prefer an arrangement that forces everyone to save more, since people might be more willing to save if they know others will also do so. Thus, even if each individual, acting in isolation, saves 5 percent of his income, it is theoretically possible that each prefers a state in which everybody is compelled to save 10 percent. Such an "isolation paradox" will imply that the CRI should be less than the PRI. Of course, under certain circumstances, such as those devised in Lind (1964) and Sen (1967), this will not be true. Those conditions obtain when (1) the benefits from the savings of each individual accrue entirely to his heirs, and (2) the weight placed by each person on his own current consumption relative to the weight he attaches to the future consumption of his heirs equals the relative weights that others place on his current consumption and on the consumption of his heirs. But even if the second condition (which is a rather strong assumption) holds, the first condition is quite unlikely to hold, if only because of taxation. If the first condition does not hold, the CRI will be less than the market interest rate whenever individuals value their own consumption more highly than that of others. The Sen–Marglin argument that the CRI should be regarded as less than the market interest rate, therefore, is not implausible.

There is another way of looking at the market interest rate and the social discount rate. Even in perfect capital markets, the market rate of interest indicates the relative weights people attach to their own consumption in different years, which is to say, at different ages. Comparisons of generally distributed benefits over time, however, require the comparisons of generally distributed benefits accruing to representative people at different times, such as an average thirty-year-old this year versus an average thirty-year-old next year. Comparisons of the marginal utility of consumption to the same age group in different years requires direct welfare judgments.[2]

2. This argument underlies the CRI formulation in Little and Mirrlees (1974). The exposition below was suggested to the author by Professor Mirrlees.

To illustrate, consider three individuals A, B, and C, each with a two-year life span. Let dz (A, 1982) be the increment in consumption A receives in 1982; similarly define dz (A, 1983), dz (B, 1983), dz (B, 1984), and dz (C, 1984), and dz (C, 1985). The two types of comparisons are indicated in the diagram—the broken lines refer to comparisons through the market interest rate and the solid lines refer to intergenerational comparisons through the CRI:

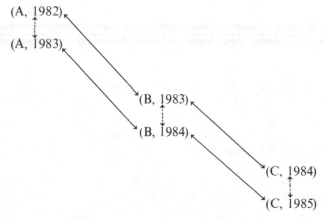

More formally, assume for simplicity that dz is the same for all individuals in all years, except that dz (A, 1982) = dz (C, 1985) = 0. Then the social welfare change can be written as

$$dW = \alpha_{83} U'(A, 83)dz + \alpha_{83} U'(B, 83)dz$$
$$+ \alpha_{84} U'(B, 84)dz + \alpha_{84} U'(C, 84)dz$$

with α as the welfare weight, and U' (A, 83) as the marginal utility of dz to A in 1983, and so on. Note also that

$$R \equiv (1 + r) = \frac{U'(A, 82)}{U'(A, 83)} = \frac{U'(B, 83)}{U'(B, 84)} = \frac{U'(C, 84)}{U'(C, 85)},$$

where r is the market interest rate, which is assumed constant and common to all individuals. Similarly, define

$$Q \equiv \frac{U'(A, 82)}{U'(B, 83)} = \frac{U'(B, 83)}{U'(C, 84)},$$

the ratio of marginal utilities of different individuals at the same age. Q is also assumed constant for simplicity.

One can therefore rewrite

$$dW = X dz + Y dz,$$

where
$$X = \alpha_{83} U'(A, 82)/R + \alpha_{83} U'(B, 83)$$
$$= \alpha_{83} U'(B, 83)[(Q + R)/R]$$

and
$$Y = \alpha_{84} U'(B, 83)/R + \alpha_{84} U'(C, 84)$$
$$= \alpha_{84} U'(C, 84)[(Q + R)/R].$$

Then,
$$1 + \text{CRI} = X/Y = \alpha_{83} U'(B, 83)/\alpha_{84} U'(C, 84)$$
$$= (\alpha_{83}/\alpha_{84})Q = (1 + \rho)Q$$

with ρ being the social time preference rate.

Now Q may be defined as $1 + \eta g$; g indicating how B's income in 1983 differs from A's in 1982, and so on, and η indicating the diminishing social weights on higher incomes. Then

$$1 + \text{CRI} = (1 + \rho)(1 + \eta g) \cong 1 + \rho + \eta g,$$
and
$$\text{CRI} = \eta g + \rho.$$

Since the term R, incorporating the market interest rate, does not appear in the CRI expression, this example illustrates that the market interest rate may have no effect on the intergenerational comparisons involved in defining the CRI. It can be seen from above that heroic assumptions would be needed to justify defining CRI as the market interest rate. This is after all what one should expect, since the questions being asked are different —the market interest rate refers to life-cycle allocations and the CRI refers to intergenerational allocations.

At the same time, defining CRI as above does not mean that market interest rates are irrelevant to cost-benefit analysis. The view that the Little–Mirrlees approach necessarily disregards market interest rates is both widely held and erroneous. When the CRI is used to discount a project's cost-benefit stream, it is implicitly assumed that the incidence of costs and benefits are generally distributed across different age groups. If, to take an extreme example, the project affected a single individual, the net present value of his gains (at his own interest rate) should count. It will then be socially weighted —not only by the income distribution weight but also by the shadow price of investment, which is discussed next.

Shadow Pricing of Investment

As this discussion suggests, there does not appear to be a compelling case for regarding the CRI as the PRI. But even if these rates of interest were assumed to be equal, their equality with the marginal returns to investment in efficiency prices cannot be taken for granted. This section discusses how a difference between these rates of interest would affect cost-benefit analysis.

To begin, assume that they are equal. The standard net present value expression for a project is then

$$N = \sum_{t=0}^{T} \frac{B_t - C_t}{(1 + i)^t}.$$

With CRI $\equiv i \equiv$ IRI, B_t and C_t are benefits and costs, measured in efficiency prices, as compared with the "without project" alternative. Aggregate consumption is the numeraire, the welfare measures being normalized with respect to the value of private consumption expenditures at market prices.

The methods of project financing are (1) additional taxation (including increases in the prices of public sector services), (2) borrowing from the domestic capital market, and (3) curtailment of other public sector expenditures, including investment and noninvestment expenditures (government "consumption" is difficult to define). Financial deficits in any year, including the early years, can be financed in these ways or financial surpluses can be disposed of correspondingly. Foreign borrowing and lending is another alternative that may be relevant.

These financial policies, together with the distribution policies pertaining to project benefits (B_t), including user charges or prices, quantity allocation rules, and direct selection of beneficiaries, determine the distributional features of a project. In general, the project's distributional impact is likely to fall on four broad categories of expenditures: public investment, public non-investment expenditures, private investment, and private consumption. Suppose the benefits are distributed among these four groups in proportions b_1, b_2, b_3, b_4 (with $\sum b_i = 1$). Similarly, the costs may be distributed among these four groups in proportions, c_i (with $\sum c_i = 1$). The NPV of a project can be written accordingly, replacing $(B_t - C_t)$ with $(\sum b_{it} B_t - \sum c_{it} C_t)$. Financial arrangements are implicit in this form, which is broader than that in Feldstein (1973).

This formulation assumes that the marginal value of all these expenditures, in relation to the value of a unit of private consumption, is unity. For example, one unit of public investment produces a stream of consumption benefits (whether or not reinvestment takes place) whose present value, at the CRI, is one. The returns to public and private investments must, of course, be equal for this to be true.

Suppose now that the efficiency rate of return, IRI, is different for public and private sector investments: r_1 for public and r_2 for private. Moreover, assume that both r_1 and r_2 exceed the CRI. Let G be the present value of a unit of public investment and P the present value of a unit of private investment, both in relation to consumption at domestic prices. For simplicity, one may assume that noninvestment public expenditures have the same value as public investments. Let b_1, b_2, b_3 be the shares of private consumption, private investment, and public investment in the project benefits created, and let c_1, c_2, c_3 be their corresponding shares in project costs. The latter depend on whether the project displaces other public expenditures only, or private investment and consumption as well. The NPV criterion now becomes

$$N = \sum_{t=0}^{T} \frac{(b_{1t} + P_t b_{2t} + G_t b_{3t}) B_t - (c_{1t} + P_t c_{2t} + G_t c_{3t}) C_t}{(1+i)^t}.$$

The NPV rule will simplify to the standard one only if the weighted shares of benefits and costs are equal and constant in all years,[3] a condition that can hardly be true in practice.

The calculations of the shadow prices G and P can be quite complex, since they depend not only on the yields on public and private investments but also on how these yields are distributed between consumption, reinvestment, and public income. Analysts concerned with their estimation can devise their own formulas depending on the precision needed or feasible in the light of available information. For the present purpose, it will suffice to focus on two relatively simple special cases, both assuming $G = P$, which are also sometimes used to derive crude estimates.[4]

Case 1. If a project displaces public or private investments, and if the returns from these forgone investments would have been consumed entirely, then the present value of their benefits is given by

$$\sum_{t=1}^{T} \frac{B_t}{(1 + i)^t}.$$

Suppose, for example, that the costs of a project, K_0, are incurred entirely in the initial year. If K_0 were invested elsewhere with a yield of $(1 + r)$ in year 1 and zero yields thereafter, the benefit sacrificed in using K_0 in this project rather than elsewhere is $K_0[(1 + r)/(1 + i)]$. More generally, if r is defined as the returns net of depreciation and expenditures needed to maintain the initial capital stock perpetually, if it is constant over time, and if it is consumed rather than reinvested, then $G = P = r/i$. To the extent that reinvestments occur, G and P will clearly be underestimated by this shortcut method.

Case 2. Reinvestments can be allowed for in a simple way if the fraction of the benefits from displaced investments is constant, say, s, and if i and r are also constant. Then $G = P = (1 - s)r/(i - sr)$, a formula that works as long as i and sr are not close to each other.

If G and P differ, optimal allocation of investments between the public and the private sectors does not require equality of the yields, r_1 and r_2, as in the traditional approach, since lower productivity in, say, the public sector can be offset by a higher propensity to reinvest.

The shadow price of investments, compared with consumption, can also be interpreted in terms of its role in equating the demand for investment funds with its supply. This can be done for the economy as a whole or for the public and private sectors separately. This illustration focuses only on the

3. Then the common factor $(b_1 + P \cdot b_2 + G \cdot b_3)$ will merely adjust the scale of the NPV without affecting its sign.

4. Dasgupta, Marglin, and Sen (1972), Little and Mirrlees (1974), and Squire and van der Tak (1975) all discuss these and other methods for estimating G.

public sector's budget. Suppose that the returns to private investments equal the CRI (so that $P = 1$), whereas the returns to public investments exceed the CRI. This assumption implies that public investment should be expanded. Thus, if one evaluates one unit of public investment at the margin by using a shadow price of unity, its net present value will be positive. That is,

$$N = \sum_{1}^{\infty} \frac{sr + (1 - s)r}{(1 + i)^t} - 1 > 0,$$

where s and r refer to the public sector only and are assumed constant over time.

One can now define G^* such that the marginal project's net present value becomes zero when the investment component is evaluated at that shadow price. That is,

$$N = \sum_{1}^{\infty} \frac{srG^* + (1 - s)r}{(1 + i)^t} - G^* = 0,$$

or

$$\frac{srG^*}{i} + \frac{(1 - s)r}{i} - G^* = 0.$$

Solving for G^*, which can always be found if $i \neq sr$,

$$G^* = \frac{(1 - s)r}{i - sr},$$

which is precisely the value of G defined in Case II above. Thus, in combination with the CRI, the shadow price of public investment is defined in such a way as to make the marginal net benefits from public investment zero, so that neither expansion nor contraction is desired: the budget balances.

The value of G that balances the public budget may, of course, vary from year to year. Nevertheless, if it can be assumed that at some future date, T, the value of public investment will equal that of consumption, and if in addition a constant rate of fall of G is assumed until year T, the values of G for all years, including the current one, can be readily determined by working backwards.

The Harberger Method

In an influential article, Harberger (1976, Chap. 4) proposed the use of a discount rate, defined as an average of r and CRI, as an alternative to the approach described above. In this approach, the discount rate for cost-benefit analysis, ω, is defined as

$$\omega = \theta \bar{r} + (1 - \theta)\bar{i},$$

where $\bar{r}$ is an average of separate marginal gross-of-tax returns to capital in the private sector, weighted by interest elasticities of investment demand; i is an average of separate net-of-personal-tax yields on savings (that is, of separate PRI's), weighted by interest elasticities of savings; θ is the fraction of public funds displacing private investments when the government borrows from the capital market; and $(1 - \theta)$ is the corresponding fraction displacing private consumption.

Harberger assumes in this method that public investments are financed by borrowing from a perfect (although distorted) capital market and that there is full employment in the economy. In the special case in which savings are completely interest inelastic, $\theta = 1, \omega = \bar{r}$. The discount rate can then be calculated directly from estimates of the private sector returns to investment, an assumption that simplifies actual empirical work (Harberger, 1976, Chap. 6).

To relate this approach to the previous one, suppose that each unit of public investment is financed by displacing θ units of private investment and $(1 - \theta)$ units of consumption. A unit of private investment has a perpetual gross-of-tax yield of r which is fully consumed. Its present value, therefore, is $P = r/i$, where i is the social (and private) consumption rate of interest. If, at the margin, public investment yields a perpetual (and constant) stream of δ, then its net present value would be

$$\delta/i - [(1 - \theta) + \theta P] = V.$$

If $V \geq 0$, then so also is $\delta/(i\alpha) \quad 1 = V/\alpha$, where $\alpha - (1 - \theta) + \theta P$. Thus, the factor $i\alpha$ may be regarded as the effective discount rate. It equals ω, the "average" discount rate suggested by Harberger since

$$i\alpha = (1 - \theta)i + \theta r \equiv \omega.$$

This approach, and its relation to the shadow pricing of investment method, has been discussed at length in Feldstein (1973) and Sjaastad and Weiscarver (1979). The main concern is reinvestments. It can easily be seen that if the investments displaced by a project would have led to reinvestments or if the marginal public sector project leads to reinvestments, then the effective discount rate is no longer ω. Assume that public investment at the margin yields δ as before, but $s\delta$ is reinvested. The net present value of the marginal project is then

$$\frac{(1 - s)\delta}{i} + \frac{s\delta G}{i} - [(1 - \theta) + \theta P] = V,$$

with
$$P = \frac{(1 - s)r}{(i - sr)} = G.$$

In this case, the previous weighted average formula for ω cannot be derived. If either private or public investments, or both, give rise to reinvestments of project profits, this approach becomes imprecise.

Nonetheless, the Harberger approach to this issue in cost-benefit analysis is the simplest one to use. The complexities of using the shadow-pricing-of-investment method will become evident from the following discussion of the Little–Mirrlees–Squire–van der Tak variant.

The Little–Mirrlees–Squire–van der Tak (LMST) Method

The LMST technique is essentially the same as the shadow-pricing-of-investment method discussed earlier, but with two adjustments. First, all values are expressed in terms of foreign exchange (as discussed in Chapter 4). Second, all values are expressed in relation to the marginal value of investments, rather than consumption. Since the values of public and private investments might differ, the numeraire is defined more narrowly to include only public expenditures. It could be narrowed further if the value of public investments is seen as different from the value of other public expenditures. The exact definition is a matter of preference and convenience since, as long as consistency is maintained throughout the analysis, nothing of substance is involved. But if all values are defined in terms of foreign exchange and uncommitted public income, the net present value of a project of, say, Rs100 million, would be worth exactly as much as a grant of Rs100 million of foreign currencies (at the official exchange rate) to the government of the country concerned. The LMST adjustments should therefore have considerable intuitive and presentational appeal to decisionmakers in developing countries. These adjustments, which are fairly complex, are made explicit below.

Suppose that in Year 0, a project increases welfare by increasing both private and public incomes. The effects on welfare stem from direct changes in consumption in Year 0 and from changes in consumption in current and future years induced by private investments and public expenditures. The former effect may be written as

$$\sum_{j=1} w_j dC_{j0},$$

where w_j is the social utility of person j's gain, dC_{j0}. Let W_p be the present value, in "utils," of the net consumption stream resulting from a unit of private investment, dI_p, and similarly let W_g be the net present value of a unit of public expenditures, dI_g. The net change in welfare during Year 0 can then be written, in "utils," as

$$dW = \sum w_j dC_{j0} + W_p dI_p + W_g dI_g.$$

If it is assumed that $w_j = w_i = w$, all i and j, then aggregate consumption can be used as the numeraire, that is

$$dW_1 = dW/w = \sum dC_{j0} + P dI_p + G dI_g,$$

with $P \equiv W_p/w$, $G \equiv W_g/w$. P and G are the shadow prices of private and public expenditures, in relation to the consumption numeraire, used earlier.

Alternatively, one can use public income as the numeraire, as in Little–Mirrlees:

$$dW_2 \equiv dW_1/G = \frac{\sum dC_{j0}}{G} + \frac{P}{G} dI_p + dI_g.$$

This completes one step in the process. But all values must still be expressed in units equivalent to foreign exchange by using conversion factors, along the lines discussed in Chapter 4. The use of the foreign exchange numeraire, however, implies that all the parameters discussed earlier must be redefined. For example, the CRI might then be redefined, as in Little–Mirrlees, to compare current and future consumption benefits in border prices, rather than in domestic prices, and its value may differ if the conversion factor for current consumption differs from that for future consumption. For the conversion factor to remain constant, the incidence of taxes and tariffs and the pattern of marginal expenditures must remain unchanged. Similarly, the costs and benefits of public and private investment expenditures should be evaluated also at border prices; thus, IRI may change when redefined in border prices. The optimality condition is the same, however: IRI = CRI in the traditional and the Dasgupta, Marglin, and Sen approaches, and $q = \widehat{CRI}$ in the Little–Mirrlees approach, q and $\widehat{CRI}$ being the same as IRI and CRI except that their values are expressed in terms of border prices. The redefinition in terms of border prices allows, moreover, a direct comparison of the marginal cost of borrowing with the return to investment. For, if f is the marginal cost (benefit) of foreign borrowing (lending), then optimality requires that $q = \widehat{CRI} = f$.

Before discussing the formulas for discount rate and the shadow price of investments in this approach, it is convenient to adopt a well-defined notational system. The system used in Squire–van der Tak is somewhat more useful in practice than the system in Little–Mirrlees, since it shows more explicitly the computational steps involved.

The most important notational difference in the Squire–van der Tak system concerns the shadow price of public investments, that is, the parameter G. In Little–Mirrlees, the value of public investment in border prices is expressed in relation to the value of consumption in *border* prices—s in their notation. In the Squire–van der Tak system, the value of public investment in border prices is expressed in relation to the value of consumption in *domestic* prices. Their parameter $v \equiv s/\beta$, where β is a consumption conversion factor. Given this redefinition of the shadow price of public income, the CRI can be interpreted as in the traditional approach.

The ARI and v

The shadow price of public investments, v, is formally defined as $v \equiv W_g/W_c$, where W_c is the value, in "utils," of additional consumption at the per capita consumption level. The latter is chosen as the reference point for convenience, in case distribution weights are to be used. The discount rate in this approach must be redefined as the rate at which the numeraire, namely, the "util" value of public investment (W_g), changes over time. This discount rate, which is called the "accounting rate of interest" (ARI), is simply $- (dW_g/dt)/W_g$, assuming that this rate is constant. Thus, one can derive the definitional identity:

$$- \frac{d \log v}{dt} \equiv ARI - CRI.$$

It may be useful to confirm that this new definition of the discount rate makes no difference to the substance of the analysis. Suppose a project yields (B_0, B_1) as benefits, all consumed. The present value of the benefits is then:

$$B_0 + \frac{W_{c,1}}{W_{c,0}} B_1 = B_0 + \frac{1}{(1+i)} B_1,$$

where i is the CRI. Using the new numeraire, the present value is

$$\left(\frac{W_{c,0}}{W_{g,0}} \right) B_0 + \left(\frac{W_{c,1}}{W_{g,1}} \right) \frac{W_{g,1}}{W_{g,0}} B_1 = \frac{B_0}{v_0} + \frac{1}{v_1} \frac{B_1}{(1 + ARI)}.$$

Since nothing has been done except to multiply the former expression by $W_{c,0}/W_{g,0} = 1/v_0$, analytical results are not changed.

The ARI may be interpreted as the fully adjusted social opportunity cost of capital, taking account of the differential valuation of savings and consumption. Since the net present value of the marginal unit of investment is zero at the ARI (since v and ARI must balance the budget), the latter can be interpreted as the return to the marginal project. If the yield of the project is q (perpetuity), of which a fraction, s, is reinvested, then the relation between ARI and q is

$$ARI = sq + (1 - s)q/(\beta v).$$

The ARI will be less than q if there is a positive premium on investment $(\beta v > 1)$. If, as in the Little–Mirrlees model, consumption occurs only through wage employment, one can write

$$ARI = sq + a/\beta v,$$

where a is the consumption increment owing to employment ($c - m$ in their notation). This formulation assumes that the public sector budget is fixed; that is, a public project replaces another public project (or a set of replacements in many other public projects). If one introduces bond financing, as in Harberger, the formula will need to be changed.

Introducing distribution weights

If one introduces distribution weights, a critical consumption level (CCL) can be defined as that level of consumption at which marginal increments to public income are as valuable as marginal increments to consumption; that is, with the constant-elasticity approach,

$$d_{\text{CCL}} \equiv \left[\frac{\bar{C}}{\text{CCL}} \right]^{\eta} = \beta v = s$$

where $\bar{C}$ is the per capita consumption level, and s is the Little–Mirrlees shadow price of investment. Then

$$-\frac{d \log s}{dt} = \eta \frac{d \log \text{CCL}}{dt} - \eta \frac{d \log \bar{C}}{dt} = \text{ARI} - \text{CRI}.$$

If CRI is defined for the average group, $\bar{C}$, then

$$\text{CRI} = \eta \bar{g} + \rho, \quad \text{with} \quad \bar{g} \equiv \frac{d \log \bar{C}}{dt}.$$

Consequently,

$$\text{ARI} = \eta g_{\text{CCL}} + \rho, \quad \text{with} \quad g_{\text{CCL}} \equiv \frac{d \log \text{CCL}}{dt}.$$

Thus, if the rate of growth of the CCL can be independently predicted, ARI can also be estimated in this way. This result is intuitively obvious. Since a marginal gain at the CCL has, by definition, a social value equal to that of public income, the rate at which that value declines over time, $(- d \log W_{\text{CCL}}/dt)$, must be the same as the rate at which the value of public income $(- d \log W_g/dt)$ declines over time, and the latter is the ARI.

As will become apparent in subsequent chapters, the effective weight on any consumption gain is not d_i but d_i/v.[5] This is a composite of the consumption weights and the weight on public income. One can thus define

$$h_i = \frac{1}{v} \left(\frac{\bar{C}}{C_i} \right)^{\eta}$$

$$= \frac{1}{v} \left(\frac{\bar{C}}{\text{CCL}} \frac{\text{CCL}}{C_i} \right)^{\eta}.$$

But since $(\bar{C}/\text{CCL})^{\eta}$ equals βv,

$$h_i = \beta \left(\frac{\text{CCL}}{C_i} \right)^{\eta}.$$

5. The weights are defined as in Chapter 3, $d_i = (\bar{C}/C_i)^{\eta}$.

This composite weighting function makes no reference to the per capita consumption level, $\bar{C}$. This is the reason the choice of $\bar{C}$, or of some other reference point, is immaterial. What really matters is the choice of the CCL, since it fixes the actual weights used in the analysis.[6]

Estimation

By now numerous studies have attempted to estimate the various parameters discussed. The extent of work on which their estimation is based varies considerably—often the estimates are made in an extremely crude fashion, with a noticeable tendency to arrive at noncontroversial results. An assessment of the degree to which particular studies have produced reliable results is extremely difficult and is not attempted here. Instead, the main types of issues that arise in this context are discussed below, with references to a sample of the empirical literature.

The marginal return to investments measured in efficiency prices is often estimated on an economywide basis, using aggregate production functions (see, for example, Linn, 1977, and Mashayekhi, 1980). Estimates tend to lie in the 8–12 percent range, although higher figures are occasionally suggested for fast-growing economies such as Korea. These estimates are not particularly sensitive to the use of border prices, so that one can regard IRI $= q$ for all practical purposes.

As distinct from economywide estimates, separate estimates for public and private sectors are less frequently available. Estimates of public sector returns are usually based on cash returns only. Cash returns, however, are not relevant for the non-revenue-generating investments frequently undertaken in the public sector. Since such investments may often have high payoffs—for example, highway construction and maintenance—the exclusion of such investments tends to seriously bias the results downward. Moreover, cash returns often understate the benefits from large investments in the revenue-generating sectors as well, especially when, as in many public utilities, tariffs are maintained at low levels. Not surprisingly, estimates of public sector returns are often very low. Authors generally prefer, therefore, to use either an economywide estimate or a separate estimate of private sector returns.[7] Occasionally, the estimate of q is based on returns to the sector considered to be most important at the margin—such as

---

6. In the terminology of Little–Mirrlees, the composite function is simply $w_i = (b/C_i)^\eta$, where b is the CCL in border prices and C_i is also measured in border prices.

7. For an excellent example of the estimation of both economywide and separate sectoral returns, see Harberger (1976, Chap. 6). His estimate of the public sector return of 2 percent for Colombia is about the same as the return in Pakistan estimated by Squire, Little, and Durdag (1979); both reflect the problems indicated above.

manufacturing—without distinguishing between public and private operations (see Lal, 1980).

In countries with a narrow range of public investments, direct experience with project work may often substitute for, or at least provide a cross-check to, economywide estimates. In small economies with poor resource endowments, the history of project work may suggest, for example, that investments yielding more than 6 or 7 percent are very difficult to identify at the margin—the higher yielding projects being already included in aid packages of donor countries. Acceptance of low estimates for q may not be inappropriate in such cases.[8]

In regard to the CRI, it has been noted earlier that the specification of η and ρ represents value judgments, which are implicitly or explicitly involved in all cost-benefit methodologies, including the traditional one. Those using the constant-elasticity form tend to set η values in the range of 1–3, with most preferring values on the low side.

If η is chosen as 1 or 2, the CRI must be quite low, since few developing countries can expect a per capita rate of growth in consumption much over 2 percent over a long period. It is common practice, however, to introduce a positive time preference rate (ρ), in the 2–5 percent range, thus driving up the value of the CRI. The rationale for doing so may be illustrated by two examples. Squire, Little, and Durdag (1979) proceed as follows:

> Pakistan's draft Fifth Plan makes it quite clear that growth is the primary aim of the next few years, although equity is not neglected. This suggests a zero or very low value for the rate of pure time preference (0–1%), because an increase in this parameter reduces, other things being equal, the extent to which the weighting system favours growth. It also suggests a positive, but not large, value for the social elasticity of the marginal utility of consumption (η). It must be positive in order to reflect some degree of concern for income distribution. But it should not be taken to be very large, since the higher its value, the higher is the consumption rate of interest.

They proceed to set $\eta = 2$, $\rho = 0$, which yields a CRI of 3 percent for Pakistan.

In a contrasting approach, Scott (1977) chooses $\eta = 1.5$ and $\rho = 1.5$ for Great Britain. He proceeds in two steps. First, he postulates that individuals equate the market interest rate to $\eta_{\bar{g}} + \rho$, where $\bar{g}$ is the per capita growth rate in consumption—the individuals are assumed to be socially conscious to the extent that they use $\bar{g}$ in guiding their behavior rather than their own

8. It is sometimes suggested that the returns to past World Bank–financed projects might be used as a guide, perhaps because such projects are typically thoroughly analyzed. Since the expected returns from Bank projects are often of the order of 20 percent or more, however, they are unlikely to be a useful guide.

life-cycle data. Second, he studies the real net-of-tax yield on Consols (long-term government securities) to infer the long-term rate of discount of private citizens. Given estimates of the real yields for different periods in the past (the yields ranged from 2.13 to 4.57), he experiments with pairs of values of η and ρ to fit the equation $\eta_{\hat{g}} + \rho = $ yield, choosing $\eta = 1.5$ and $\rho = 0.5$ as the best pair. Finally, he increases his estimate of ρ to 1.5 because the "risk of total destruction of our society has increased" compared with the earlier periods studied.

The estimation of the ARI, like that of q, is often quite difficult. Given that $q > $ ARI if there is an investment premium, and ARI $ > $ CRI if that premium is expected to fall at all, one can set limits to the value of the ARI. But this is not of much help, since the difference between q and CRI can still be wide, say, 5 to 8 percent. More useful are judgments on how fast the investment premium might fall in the medium term. If it is not expected to fall by very much—and this is typically assumed in the actual evaluation of projects— then it should be set close to the CRI.

In principle, one might also calculate the marginal cost (benefit) of foreign borrowing (lending), f, and set the ARI at that value. In fact, ARI $ = f$ is the condition that must be met if the level of foreign borrowing or lending is optimal. But the marginal cost of borrowing in real terms has been quite low, at least until recently, for countries that have access to foreign capital at international interest rates. This suggests that the level of borrowing has been suboptimal or, alternatively, foreign loans have been "rationed" so that the true cost exceeds the apparent marginal cost. In any case, the apparent marginal borrowing cost could not be used as a meaningful estimate of the ARI, although the situation might well change in the future.

In the absence of such a convenient guide, the ARI is typically estimated as $sq + (1 - s)q/(\beta v)$. As such, it is a function of v, for which another equation is needed. An alternative form of this expression can be obtained if the ARI is interpreted as the return to industrial investments and if the consumption changes owing to those investments are entirely attributable to industrial employment, as in Lal (1980). Then

$$\text{ARI} = s_{\hat{q}} + w(1 - k),$$

where $\hat{q}$ is the rate of return in efficiency prices, excluding the cost of labor; w is the fraction of that return consumed; and k is the ratio of the shadow wage rate to the market wage rate. In this case, the parameter v enters indirectly through k.

The most popular equation for estimating v is simply the Case I equation described earlier, $v = q/(\beta$ CRI$)$, which usually implies a value of v of the order of 2.5. In principle, this equation is not consistent with the ARI equation described above, since the latter allows for reinvestment while the former does not. But given that the neglect of reinvestments will underestimate v, using it to derive the ARI will produce an overestimate, other things being equal. Most people prefer to bias the estimate this way, rather than take the risk of significantly underestimating the ARI. And this risk is considerable if the Case II equation for v is used instead, since i and sq might be quite close.

The troubles with the Case II equation stem from the assumed constancy of the parameters over time. One can, in principle, do much better. For example, if one can identify and analyze the marginal set of public investment projects—not totally inconceivable in practice—then one can estimate v from

$$\text{NPV} = 0 = \sum_{t=0}^{T} \left(\sum_{i} w_{it} R_t + v_t s_t R_t \right) \bigg/ (1 + i)^t - \sum_{t=0}^{T} \frac{v_t K_t}{(1 + i)^t},$$

where
R_t = returns, gross of depreciation, in border prices
K_t = costs in border prices
v_t = shadow price of investments
$s_t R_t$ = fraction of R_t saved
$w_{it} = d_{it} c_{it}/\beta_t$, where c_{it} is the consumption in border prices per unit of returns of group i at time t, β_t are consumption conversion factors, and d_{it} are consumption weights for group i at time t.

To check the consistency of this with earlier formulas, assume that

$$\sum_{i} d_{it} c_{it}/\beta_t \simeq \sum_{i} d_i c_i/\beta = (1 - s)/\beta,$$

$$K_0 = 1, \quad K_t = 0 \quad \text{for} \quad t > 0,$$

$$s_t R_t = sR,$$

the value of terminal assets is zero, and

$$v_t = v_0,$$

then
$$v_0 = \frac{(1 - s) R\theta}{\beta(1 - sr\theta)},$$

with
$$\theta \equiv \sum_{0}^{T} \frac{1}{(1 + i)^t}.$$

The Case II equation is obtained as $T \to \infty$.

This more general formulation indicates that one can do better, in principle, if one knows enough to relax one or more of the special assumptions required to derive the Case II equation. It is also clear that if either the Case I or the Case II equation is used, it is assumed that v is constant over time, in which case ARI = CRI, and the $sq + (1 - s)q/(\beta v)$

equation takes the role of an independent check on the initial specification of the CRI.[9]

If one does not assume a specific rate of change in v, the formulation above cannot be used to solve for v_0, the initial value of v. There will in that case be two unknowns, v_0 and its rate of change (or more than two if the rate of change itself is allowed to vary). The two unknowns would be v and ARI, since the latter is determined by the rate of change in v (given CRI).

The Little–Mirrlees approach suggests, as a simplification, that the rate of change in v be assumed constant and that a planned date, T, should be postulated at which the investment premium will disappear ($\beta v = 1$). In that case, they show that

$$v_0 = \frac{1}{\beta}[1 + \tfrac{1}{2}(\text{ARI} - \text{CRI})]^T.$$

This equation can be used to complete the system, but it requires the specification of T exogenously, which is difficult to do. For example, Lal (1980), in setting $T = 50$ for India, assumed that by that date gross domestic savings would be 37 percent of GNP, the same as in Japan in 1969, if the projections in the Fifth Plan were linearly extrapolated. His rationale for using either the Japanese performance as a guide or for extrapolating plan projections for 1985–86 (which was 20 percent) is not, however, altogether clear. If the U.S. performance is taken as a guide instead, for example, then T will have been attained by 1985–86. Since the value of v is quite sensitive to the choice of T, and since a good basis for choosing T is hard to find, it is not clear that this approach offers significant advantages over the much cruder approach of using $v = q/(\beta \, \text{CRI})$, and then $\text{ARI} = sq + (1 - s)q/(\beta v)$, the difference between the ARI thus estimated and the CRI being the implied rate of change in v.

Another line of attack involves attempts at independent estimates of the critical consumption level (CCL). Since the value of consumption gains at the CCL equals v, knowledge of CCL implies knowledge of v, and vice versa. If the behavior of a government does, in fact, mirror the basic assumptions of analysis, then the CCL may be regarded as the threshold income above which persons would be taxed and below which persons would be subsidized, were lump-sum transfers feasible. Thus, analysts have often referred to the income tax threshold as a maximum value for the CCL. Of course, the CCL could be somewhat below this income tax threshold because of the negative incentive effects of taxation. The CCL might also be somewhat above that threshold if the cost of taxing persons below the CCL is less than the gains from lowering the marginal tax rates on those above the

---

9. The question $\text{ARI} = sq + (1 - s)q/(\beta v)$ yields the current period ARI as a function of the current period v and does not, by itself, imply that v is constant over time.

CCL. It is, nonetheless, plausible that the maximum value of the CCL will lie within a reasonably small neighborhood of the income tax threshold.

That threshold yields an upper bound. It is quite conceivable that the CCL will be much less than that threshold. If there existed another clear line above which income subsidies stopped, then such a line could similarly be regarded as an approximate lower bound. It is, however, much more difficult to find such a line in developing countries. Since "absolute poverty" lines have been estimated for many countries, such a line is an obvious candidate. The very definition of absolute poverty tends to suggest eligibility for subsidies. However, in countries in which a large fraction of the population is below that line, the use of that line for this purpose will imply either a very low value of v or a very high value of η.[10] Even when the poverty line is a plausible lower bound, the gap between the upper and lower bounds can be quite wide. For example, the upper bound might be 40 percent of the per capita income, while the lower bound is only 25 percent. Such a range implies, as orders of magnitude, $2.5 \leq v \leq 4$ if $\eta = 1$, and $6.3 \leq v \leq 16$ if $\eta = 2$.[11]

Nonetheless, attempts to estimate the CCL independently, or to check the plausibility of its value implied by the estimate of v, should be regarded as an important part of the exercise. In fact, this approach can sometimes be very useful. For example, Scott (1977) regards the maximum level of income at which eligibility for supplementary benefits occurs as the CCL for the United Kingdom. If one shares this opinion, one can both obtain a value of v and infer the ARI from the rate of growth of the eligibility line, which is what Scott does, using the equation discussed earlier: $\text{ARI} = \eta\, g_{\text{CCL}} + \rho$. The problems of estimating v and ARI are simultaneously solved by this device.

As this discussion of the CCL suggests, one might try to estimate v as the marginal social benefit from public sector expenditures other than investments. For example, since food subsidies are common in developing countries, such subsidies might be analyzed to discover the implied value of v. Thus, suppose that the amount of income transferred to group i is S_i, and $\beta_i S_i$ in border prices, then the value of the subsidy should be zero at the optimum:

$$\sum_i \frac{d_i S_i}{v} - \sum \beta_i S_i = 0,$$

10. Another way of checking the plausibility of using this line as the CCL is to substitute v by CCL in the equation relating v to T. That equation can then be solved for T. Thus, Lal (1980) finds that the commonly used absolute poverty line is an implausible value for India, since it implies $T = 5$!

11. In theory, the CCL may even lie below any observed income level—if the income dispersion is low and v is high. This occurs in the first phase of the growth model analyzed by Anand (1981). The government should then be concerned only with maximizing growth, until transfers become desirable in later phases.

yielding $\qquad v = \dfrac{\sum d_i S_i}{\sum \beta_i S_i} = $ marginal social benefit per unit of transfer.

If such transfers are discriminatory, or if they involve measurable incentive effects and administrative costs, the formula can easily be generalized. Moreover, the policy need not be judged optimal; if the policy is regarded as too generous or too strict, one gets upper or lower bounds on v, which may still be useful.

There are very few examples of analysis of this type.[12] One reason might be that such subsidies could be rigidly linked to specific financing schemes, in which case those, too, must be introduced into the analysis. For example, if a government subsidizes food in urban areas and combines this policy with food procurement at artificially low prices, then the social costs and benefits of the procurement policy must also be taken into account in assessing the policy as a whole. As another example, the income tax schedule itself may be analyzed, but in that case it has to be viewed as a combination of tax and subsidy schemes (see Layard, 1980).

The same considerations apply also to the revenue side. The marginal social cost of obtaining a unit of resources, measured in foreign exchange, should also equal v. Thus, for a revenue-generating policy, one can write (ignoring private savings and administrative costs):

$$-\sum_i d_i(R_i - \delta_i) + v \sum \beta_i R_i = 0,$$

where $\sum_i R_i$ is the revenue raised through the policy, $\sum_i \beta_i R_i$ is its foreign exchange value, and δ_i is the deadweight loss borne by group i. Thus,

$$v = \frac{\sum_i d_i(R_i - \delta_i)}{\sum_i \beta_i R_i}.$$

With optimal policies, all v's on the revenue side and all v's on the expenditure side should be equal. If marginal social benefits exceed marginal social costs, expenditures should be expanded, and conversely, if benefits are less than costs, expenditures should be curtailed. The estimation of v has typically focused on the expenditure side, but the revenue-raising policies might conceivably be easier to analyze in some countries. If, for example, one can reasonably assume that, at the margin, all public expenditures are financed by borrowing, as in Harberger (1976, Chap. 4), or by taxation of a particular type, then one can focus on that policy to infer

12. For exceptions, see Squire, Little, and Durdag (1979) and Page (1982).

v. The reason for ignoring the revenue side is the assumption, implicit in most of the literature, that an absolute revenue constraint operates and that the social gain from reducing revenues (the v on the revenue side) is less than the social benefits forgone by reducing expenditures (the v on the expenditure side).

Since v can be interpreted in this way, the premium will never completely disappear, even by the planned date, T, of the Little–Mirrlees approach. Moreover, the need for using differential distribution weights will always remain if it is desirable in the first place. As long as lump-sum taxation remains infeasible, even strongly progressive weighting systems will continue to imply a fairly wide spread of incomes and distribution weights. This is because the cost of a subsidy program is not simply the deadweight losses incurred, but also the leakages into "nondeserving" groups which inevitably occur when perfect discrimination is not possible (see Layard, 1980).

No theory exists regarding changes in the degree of progressivity in the evaluation function over time. In its absence, it is customary to use a constant η, rather than correlate it with such features of the economy as the existing degree of inequality. The allocation of public expenditures, the design of taxes and subsidies, and the types of poverty redressal schemes may of course vary with the state of the economy, but the evaluation function itself is typically considered a fundamental constant.

The next two chapters discuss some practical aspects of the LMST system.

List of formulas

For easy reference, a list of the main formulas discussed in this chapter is provided here, using the Squire–van der Tak notational system wherever possible.

Distribution weights

Choosing the per capita consumption level in domestic prices $(\bar{C})$ as the reference point, the distribution weight, d_{it}, for group i with consumption level C_{it} at time t is:

$$d_{it} = \left(\frac{\bar{C}_t}{C_{it}} \right)^{\eta}. \tag{5.1a}$$

The parameter η is the elasticity of the marginal utility of consumption (see Chapter 3).

As an alternative, the composite weight, $d/v \equiv h$, can be obtained from

$$h_{it} = \beta_t \left(\frac{\text{CCL}}{C_i} \right)^{\eta}, \tag{5.1b}$$

the CCL being the critical consumption level, defined as that level, C_i, at which $d_{it} = \beta_t v_t$.

The discount rate

If q = returns, net of depreciation, in efficiency prices (defined in terms of border values), and s = the fraction of q reinvested, then

$$\text{ARI} = sq + (1 - s)q/(\beta v). \tag{5.2a}$$

Alternatively, if foreign borrowing is optimal,

$$\text{ARI} = f, \tag{5.2b}$$

where f is the real marginal cost of borrowing from abroad.
Alternatively,

$$\text{ARI} \equiv \text{CRI} - d \log v/dt. \tag{5.2c}$$

Alternatively, if g_{CCL} is the expected growth rate of the CCL,

$$\text{ARI} = \eta\, g_{\text{CCL}} + \rho. \tag{5.2d}$$

The shadow price of investment

Assuming that $\text{ARI} = \text{CRI}$ in year T,

$$v_0 = \frac{1}{\beta}[1 + \tfrac{1}{2}(\text{ARI} - \text{CRI})]^T. \tag{5.3a}$$

Alternatively, if v is constant,

$$v_0 = \frac{(1-s)q}{\beta(i - sq)}, \tag{5.3b}$$

where $i \equiv \text{CRI}$.
Alternatively, if $s = 0$,

$$v_0 = \frac{q}{\beta\text{CRI}}. \tag{5.3c}$$

Note that v can also be derived from the definition of the CCL if the latter is known independently.

The consumption rate of interest

The CRI is:

$$\text{CRI} = \eta\,\bar{g} + \rho, \tag{5.4a}$$

where $\bar{g}$ is the expected rate of growth of per capita income level.

Alternatively,

$$\text{CRI} = \text{PRI} = \rho^*, \tag{5.4b}$$

where ρ^* is the pure rate of private time preference. If this formulation is chosen, then $\eta = 0$ in all the formulas given above, and $\text{CRI} = $ market interest rate adjusted for marginal personal taxes on savings.

CHAPTER 6

Using Variable Weights: Techniques

GIVEN THE DIVERSITY of investment projects, one cannot assume that they affect the rate of savings in an economy, or its distribution of income, in a uniform way. Thus, the expected effects on savings and income inequality are often important elements in the overall assessment of projects, even when they are treated informally and qualitatively. Their importance is reflected in such common concerns as fiscal and financial replicability of projects, the adequacy of tariffs and cost recoveries, and the effect on poverty and employment.

As argued in Chapter 2, it is preferable to treat issues of savings and income inequality in a systematic manner if they are to be reflected in project decisions. The usual qualitative treatment of them runs the risk of serious inconsistencies—as illustrated in the earlier discussion on hybrid criteria—for two reasons. First, savings and income inequality or poverty may be defined differently by different analysts. Judgments on these concerns cannot be consistent unless uniform definitions are adopted. Second, even if the same definitions are followed by all analysts, the importance given to these concerns in different projects within the same country may vary widely. For example, different analysts may value the income increments accruing to the same beneficiaries differently. In the absence of a systematic approach, it can never be clear what judgments are really being made.

The techniques of using variable weights are discussed in this chapter. Numerical examples are used both to illustrate the techniques and to bring out some of the main practical issues one is likely to encounter. The device of using very simple examples keeps the discussion focused on essential aspects, although it cannot, of course, capture the richness of actual case studies (several of which are referred to in the next chapter).

Basic project data are presented in terms of standard economic analysis in the first section. The technique of using the investment premium is illustrated next, without bringing in distribution weights. The use of variable weights is then illustrated, and special aspects such as the nonmarginality of income changes and the time paths of distribution weights are covered. Next, a simple algebraic summary of the technique is provided. Finally, the nature of sensitivity tests in this context is discussed. The appendix presents tables of distribution weights for those who wish to experiment with their use.

Standard Analysis

The example developed below is agricultural in nature only to the extent that the project benefits are assumed to accrue to farmers. But the nature of the activity is not identified—it is not necessary to do so for the present purpose. It is simply assumed that the public sector makes an investment in Year 1 of the project, and a perpetual and constant stream of net benefits occur from Year 2 onward. Two private groups benefit from the project: the workers employed by the public sector and the farmers themselves. The public sector benefits accrue in the form of increases in tax revenues. Suppliers of inputs other than labor do not increase their profits because of the project, and the farmers and the distributors of their outputs are price-takers. There are no consumer surpluses accruing to the users of farm outputs, nor do competing producers lose. This, therefore, is a very easy case to demonstrate the use of variable distribution weights.

The farm unit, which is the focus of the example, may be thought of as a single household operation or as a set of operations by a group of homogeneous households. The farm unit is, of course, an important element in agricultural project analysis, since it enables checks on farmers' response to the project intervention and provides a sound basis for judging the choices of crop and input mixes that farmers will make. Thus, agri-

Table 1. *Financial Costs and Benefits*

Year 1		Year 2 onward	
Costs	*Rupees*	*Costs and benefits*	*Rupees*
Tradable inputs	5,500	Gross sales	1,450
Nontradable inputs		Distribution and	
Labor	4,000[a]	transport margin	60
Other	1,250	Net sales	1,390
Total incremental costs	10,750	Tradable inputs	110
		Nontradable inputs	
		Labor	160
		Other	125
		Fixed charges	95
		Total costs	490
		Net incremental benefits	
		(net sales minus total costs)	900[b]

a. Includes excess payments of Rs 800, of which consumption = Rs 760, savings = Rs 40.
b. Of which consumption = Rs 810, savings = Rs 90.

cultural project scenarios are frequently constructed on the basis of a representative set of farm models. But total project costs need not be simply the average farm-level costs times the number of farm units, and total benefits may also differ from the average benefits per farm times the number of farms. All such issues are avoided here. Nonetheless, it is worth noting that household characteristics do not matter in the standard analysis of welfare effects, since the same amount of incremental consumption is assumed to have the same social weight regardless of the size, age composition, and other features of the households involved.

The basic project data are presented in Table 1. These are all in incremental terms, comparing the "with project" with the "without project" situations. Total financial costs in Year 1 are Rs10,750, which has been decomposed into tradables, labor, and other nontradables. The net financial benefits are Rs900 a year, in perpetuity, beginning in Year 2. Its breakdown between sales, various types of inputs, and direct charges (benefit levies) are also shown. It is assumed that labor inputs are hired from a competitive market at a constant wage rate. If the project also uses family labor which would have been hired out without the project, the total number of hours worked by the family does not change, and the loss of wage income is simply substituted by income from additional production. In that case, it is not necessary to show the use of own-labor as a separate category.[1]

The corresponding economic costs and benefits are shown in Table 2, which also shows the conversion factors used. The incremental costs are Rs10,000 in Year 1, and the incremental net benefits thereafter are Rs1,000, both measured in border prices. The internal efficiency rate of return (ERR) is, therefore, 10 percent, and the net present value (NPV) is 0 at a discount rate of 10 percent. It is assumed that $q = $ CRI, as otherwise a premium or a discount on reinvestments will emerge.

In using a conversion factor of unity for gross sales, it is assumed either that the outputs are traded without trade duties or subsidies or that the particular consumption conversion factor relevant for expenditures on the farm outputs is unity. The labor conversion factors can be represented as the product of two ratios: (1) the ratio of the shadow wage rate in domestic prices to the market wage rate, and (2) the ratio of the shadow wage rate in border prices to the shadow wage rate in domestic prices. For Year 2 onward, the first is assumed to be unity; that is, the market and the shadow wage rates in domestic prices are assumed equal. The second has been

---

1. Even if the total number of hours increases, the additional own-labor can be valued at the market wage rate, and the net gain from additional work will simply be the additional income minus the cost of additional effort, valued at the market wage rate. Problems will arise only if there is no active labor market in which the family participates. In that case, the income-equivalent of additional effort cannot be so easily calculated. See the Appendix to this book for a discussion of shadow wage rates.

Table 2. *Standard Economic Costs and Benefits*

Year 1			Year 2 onward		
Costs	Conversion factors	Border rupees	Costs and benefits	Conversion factors	Border rupees
Tradable inputs	0.91	5,000	Gross sales	1.00	1,450
Nontradable inputs			Distribution and		
Labor	1.00	4,000	transport margin	0.83	50
Other	0.80	1,000	Net sales		1,400
Total incremental					
costs		10,000	Tradable inputs	0.91	100
			Nontradable inputs		
			Labor	1.25	200
			Other	0.80	100
			Total costs		400
			Net incremental		
			benefits		
			(net sales minus		
			total costs)		1,000

Note: ERR = 10 percent; NPV at 10 percent = 0; discount rate = q = CRI.

assigned a value of 1.25. This can be justified on either of two grounds: the project's use of labor diverts labor from other productive activities and their conversion factors average out at 1.25 (this can happen, for example, if labor produces exportable agricultural products subject to export taxes); or the incremental labor use comes at the expense of leisure, and the consumption conversion factor for valuing leisure is 1.25 (this can happen if the relevant consumption basket is dominated by exportables subject to trade taxes). The net result is that the shadow wage rate in border prices exceeds the market wage rate. This is not an unlikely occurrence in practice.

The conversion factor for labor used in Year 1 is similarly a product of the two ratios referred to above. As before, the second ratio has a value of 1.25, but the first is now assumed to be 0.8, since the project wage has been assumed to exceed the market wage by 25 percent. This can happen if the public sector is bound by a minimum wage law or if it hires labor without competitive bidding. The combination of these factors yields a conversion factor of unity.

Shadow Pricing of Investments

The use of the shadow price of investments is illustrated in this section. Perhaps economic rates of return or net present values are not likely to be computed without also incorporating concerns about income inequality or poverty. But there is no reason such an approach cannot be considered.

Logically, it can be regarded as a correction of the traditional form of analysis, rather than a departure from it. As discussed in Chapter 5, the need for shadow pricing investments will arise if $q >$ CRI = PRI, which can occur even if $\eta = 0$.

Moreover, most of the practical difficulties arise once one attempts to use a separate shadow price for investments. The use of variable distribution weights does, of course, require additional data and computational steps. But the extra work needed is not all that significant once the data have been prepared for using the shadow price of investments.

The simplest version of the new approach, which is adopted in the illustrations in this chapter, distinguishes only between incremental private consumption and incremental nonconsumption expenditures, whether these consist of private investments, public investments, or other types of public expenditures. Greater differentiation is frequently infeasible in practice.

Using nonconsumption expenditures as the numeraire, the undiscounted net benefits occurring during any year can be written as[2]

$$\left[\begin{array}{c} \text{Net benefits} \end{array}\right] = \left[\begin{array}{c} \text{Net benefits as in} \\ \text{standard analysis} \end{array}\right] - \left[\begin{array}{c} \text{Net social cost of} \\ \text{incremental consumption} \end{array}\right]$$

or $B = E$ $- C[\beta - (1/v)]$,

where C is the incremental value of consumption in domestic prices, v is the shadow price of investment (or of nonconsumption expenditures, as explained above), and β is the consumption conversion factor. More generally,

$$B = E - \sum_j C_j[\beta_j - (1/v)],$$

where C_j is the consumption gain of group J.

There are two consumption terms in the example considered in the previous section. In Year 1, excess wage payments were assumed to be Rs 800 (see Table 1). One would expect part of it to be saved. If 5 percent is saved, then the consumption gain is Rs 760. Thus, the net social cost of this consumption is

$$[\text{Net social cost}] = [\text{Social cost}] - [\text{Social benefit}]$$
$$= 760\beta \qquad - 760(1/v)$$
$$= 304,$$

using the values $\beta = 0.8$ and $v = 2.5$.

---

2. This form of decomposition is best explained in Squire and van der Tak (1975), pp. 52–56.

Table 3. *Economic Costs and Benefits with Investment Premium*

Year 1		Year 2 onward	
Costs	Border rupees	Net benefits	Border rupees
Costs as in Table 2	10,000	Net benefits as in Table 2	1,000
Consumption gain in		Consumption gain in	
market prices	(760)	market prices	(810)
Net cost of		Net cost of	
consumption change[a]	304	consumption change[a]	324
Total incremental costs	10,304	Incremental net benefits	676

Note: ERR = 6.6 percent. At CRI = ARI = 5 percent, NPV equals Rs3,216; at ARI = 7 percent until year 34 and ARI = 5 percent thereafter, NPV equals Rs945 if the variation in v is ignored, and is Rs2,046 with variable v.
  a. From $C(\beta - 1/v)$, where $\beta = 0.8$, $v = 2.5$.

In Year 2 and thereafter, the incremental private sector income is assumed to accrue only to the farmers, and this is Rs900. If 90 percent of this is consumed, then $C = 810$, and the net social cost of consumption is Rs324, using the same values of β and v.

Thus, as shown in Table 3, the net adjusted costs in Year 1 are Rs10,000 + Rs304 = Rs10,304. Similarly, the net adjusted benefits during Year 2 are Rs1,000 − Rs324 = Rs676. The economic rate of return is therefore only 6.7 percent. It is obvious that the introduction of the investment premium will always lower the rate of return as long as some consumption increases are induced by a project. If there are no consumption effects, then the rate of return will not change.

But the discount rate will now also be lower as long as a part of the yield from public investments leads to consumption. It is assumed here that $q = 10$ percent, as in the standard analysis, and that CRI = 5 percent. The value of $v = 2.5$ has been derived from the shortcut formula $v = q/(\beta \text{CRI})$, the merits and demerits of which were discussed at length in Chapter 5. If v is assumed to remain constant, then the relevant discount rate, ARI, is 5 percent, and the project will still be acceptable with a NPV of Rs3,216.

If v is expected to fall by, say, 2 percent per annum, then the ARI will exceed CRI until the year in which v attains its neutral value, that is, $v = 1/\beta = 1.25$. If the initial value of v is 2.5, then it will attain its neutral value in year 34 (year 34.3 to be precise). The discount rate will therefore be 7 percent until that time, and 5 percent thereafter.

If one uses the 7 percent value (until year 34), then one should, in principle, also use variable v's for calculating annual benefits. This is not usually done in practical applications, on the grounds that the gains from the extra precision are not worth the bother. In that case, the present value of the stream of annual benefits in this example can be obtained quite simply as

$$676 \sum_{t=1}^{34} (1/1.07)^t + 676 \sum_{t=34}^{\infty} (1/1.05)^t.$$

This is approximately Rs11,249. The net present value of the project is then Rs945. The project still passes the test.

If a project's NPV calculated in this way is nonnegative, and if one only wants to establish its nonnegativity, then the variability of v can be safely ignored. In a model without variable distribution weights, the annual fall in the value of v can only increase a project's NPV; it cannot lower it. But the reasons for ignoring the time path of v are not entirely convincing on *a priori* grounds. Apart from the magnitude of the rate of fall itself, the influence of its time path will depend on the project horizon and on the importance of the consumption effects of the project. Allowing for the time path can change a negative NPV into a positive one.

The influence of the time path can be readily checked in terms of the simple example being used here. The time path affects only the social benefits of the consumption change during the first 34 years. But the effect is large enough to increase the NPV of the project by about Rs1,101. This suggests that if a fast rate of fall in v is expected, the value of v should be changed frequently, say, every five years or so, even if a continuous decline is not used. Of course, the effects may be negligible for projects with short lives.

The savings of the farmers and laborers have been assigned a value equal to that of investments in this example. Suppose it were possible to evaluate their savings separately. It is not inconceivable that the incremental private savings of farmers will be reinvested on the farm rather than lent to others. If so, the value of their savings can be computed from the yields on such on-farm investments. If the shadow price of their savings, thus calculated, is p, then the basic formula given earlier should be expressed as

$$B = E - cY[\beta - (1/v)] - (1 - c)Y[\delta - (p/v)],$$

where Y is their incremental disposable income, c is their marginal propensity to consume, δ is a conversion factor for revaluing their reinvestments in border prices, and p is the shadow price of private sector investments in domestic prices relative to the value of private consumption in domestic prices.[3]

Most projects are likely to benefit several different groups. The adjustment terms can therefore be written more generally as the sum of $c_i Y_i(\beta_i - 1/v) + (1 - c_i)Y_i[\delta_i - (p_i/v)]$. The marginal propensities to con-

---

3. The term $\delta - p/v$ can alternatively be written as $\delta(1 - p^*/v)$, where p^* is the shadow price of private savings in border prices relative to the value of consumption in domestic prices.

sume, c_i, the income gains, Y_i, the conversion factors, β_i and δ_i, and the shadow price of private savings, p_i, may all vary.

In neglecting the term $\delta_1 - p_i/v$, the version of the new approach being considered here assumes, as in the traditional approach, that $\delta_i = p_i/v$. This can be appropriate only if all private savings are channeled into the same uses—by lending the savings to a general capital market, for example. Similarly, the term $\beta_i - 1/v$ can be ignored, as in traditional analysis, only if $\beta_i = 1/v$. Since in that approach v has a neutral value ($v = 1/\beta$), this assumption implies that $\beta_i = \beta$; that is, all consumption conversion factors are equal.

In principle, there is no reason to believe that $\beta_i = \beta$. This means that a transfer payment from person A to person B need not cancel out, contrary to a long-standing rule in the traditional approach. Even if Rs100 to persons A and B have the same welfare value, the real resources used by A and B in spending the sum can vary significantly. Thus, A may consume imported products with high duties (low β) and B may consume imported products with no duties ($\beta = 1$). A transfer from A to B will then increase the demand for foreign exchange.

The measurement of the consumption gains to different income groups is, however, difficult enough in most cases. Even the estimate of the marginal propensity to consume is usually derived from national accounts, although there is considerable intuitive appeal, and some evidence as well, for assuming that this propensity is higher for at least the very poor groups (see Krishna and Raychaudhuri, 1980). It is most unlikely that one should be able to differentiate β's, not to mention δ's and p's. Usually a general consumption conversion factor is used, or, failing that, a standard conversion factor.

Variable Weights

The example thus far has used only data on incremental costs and benefits. Changes in consumption can, in most cases, be more confidently predicted than its absolute levels without the project. The absolute levels must, however, be estimated if variable weights are to be used. One needs to know the consumption paths with and without the project.

The excess wage payment during the first year was assumed to be Rs800, of which Rs760 were for consumption. Let it be further assumed that this gain represents a 5 percent increase in the consumption level of that type of labor, which would have been Rs1,000 a year without the project—or one-third of the national per capita consumption level of Rs3,000 a year.[4]

---

4. Note that Rs760 and Rs810 are the total gains to all laborers and farmers, respectively. The per capita gains are assumed to be 5 percent of the per capita consumption levels.

Table 4. *Weights Used in the Illustration*

| Year 1 | Consumption level (rupees) | | | |
	Without project (a)	*National average* (b)	*Ratio* (b)/(a)	*Weights or d values*
Labor	1000	3000	3	3
Farmers	3000	3000	1	1

Similarly, let the consumption gain to farmers of Rs 810 from the second year onward be also 5 percent of what their consumption level would have been without the project—Rs 3,000 per capita a year (taking account of household size only, not its other characteristics).

If the constant-elasticity form of the valuation function is chosen, and if the elasticity of the marginal utility of income (η) is unity, then the distribution weights are simply ratios of the national per capita level to the "without project" consumption levels of the beneficiaries, as shown in Table 4.

In deriving the weights, the ratios of *income* levels may be a reasonable approximation, in most cases, for the ratios of *consumption* levels. Whether one uses ratios of consumption levels or of income levels does not matter as long as the marginal propensities to consume of the beneficiaries are not significantly different from the national average. To the extent that the propensities to consume differ, that of poor beneficiaries is likely to exceed the national average, and the use of income ratios rather than consumption ratios is likely to lead to somewhat lower weights than would be strictly correct. In practice, however, one can use income ratios to derive the weights because the errors thus introduced are likely to be quite small. Similarly, one can reasonably ignore leisure differences. The important point is that the weights, once calculated, should be used to multiply consumption changes, and not income changes, because the two might differ significantly.

Ignoring private savings, the first year costs now

$$= 10,000 + 760[\beta - (d_1/v)]$$
$$= 10,000 + 760[0.8 - (3/2.5)]$$
$$= 9,696.$$

The weighted costs are less since the incremental consumption gains of construction labor has been assigned a high value ($d_1 = 3$). This means that $(\beta - d_1/v) < 0$. In other words, that type of labor is below the critical consumption level (CCL). In the sense in which poverty is defined in this type of analysis, construction laborers are poor.

Table 5. *Economic Costs and Benefits with Variable Weights*

Year 1		Year 2 onward	
Costs	Border rupees	Net benefits	Border rupees
Costs as in Table 2	10,000	Net benefits as in Table 2	1,000
Net consumption cost (weighted value)[a]	− 304	Net consumption cost (weighted value)[b]	324
Total incremental costs	9,696	Incremental net benefits	676

a. Using $\beta = 0.8$, $v = 2.5$, $d = 3$. This cost is negative in this case.
b. Using $\beta = 0.8$, $v = 2.5$, $d = 1$.
Notes: ERR = 7 percent. At ARI = CRI = 5 percent, NPV is Rs 3,824, assuming no change in d's.

Similarly, the net benefits during the second year, and in each year thereafter, are

$$= 1,000 - 810[\beta - (d_2/v)]$$
$$= 1,000 - 810[0.8 - (1.0/2.5)]$$
$$= 676.$$

The annual net benefits decrease since the additional consumption of the farmers has a net social cost of Rs 324 a year. The farmers are clearly above the CCL. If v and the d values remain constant over time, and if ARI = CRI = 5 percent, then the NPV is Rs 3,824. The internal rate of return is about 7 percent. The basic data are summarized in Table 5.

The d values will remain constant only if the per capita consumption level of the farmers would have increased without the project at the same rate as the national per capita income level. This may not be a reasonable assumption. In many agricultural projects, the "without project" consumption levels are expected to remain constant or even decline over time—for reasons such as soil erosion, declining fertility of the land, or simply population growth in the area. The d values can therefore increase over time.

Increasing d values will enhance the effect of the falling value of v on the composite weight d/v. Neglecting the increases in this composite weight may, therefore, introduce a very serious bias in project analysis. Only if the d values are likely to fall can one reasonably ignore the time-path problem.

The increases in per capita consumption levels were assumed to be small (5 percent) in the above example. Consumption increments induced by a project are often much larger than that, especially in agricultural projects in poor areas. Increases of the order of 100 percent are not uncommon. The d values, calculated as above, cannot be used in such cases, since they are only valid for small changes. In the case of a 100 percent change, the d value

Table 6. *Nonmarginal Weights*

y parameter	*x parameter when* $\eta = 1$			*x parameter when* $\eta = 2$		
	0.1	*0.5*	*1.0*	*0.1*	*0.5*	*1.0*
0.5	1.91	1.62	1.39	3.64	2.67	2.00
1.0	0.95	0.81	0.69	0.91	0.67	0.50
2.0	0.48	0.41	0.35	0.23	0.17	0.13

Source: Appendix Tables 9 and 10.

appropriate for the last dollar may be much smaller than the d value appropriate for the first dollar.

In such cases, the d values need to be adjusted to take account of their variation over the range, as discussed in the appendix to this chapter. Some illustrative values are shown in Table 6. The parameter x indicates the change in the consumption level as a ratio of the consumption level without the project: $x = (C_2 - C_1)/C_1$, where C_1 and C_2 are the consumption levels with and without the project. Thus, $x = 1$ indicates a doubling of the consumption level. The parameter y indicates the ratio of the consumption level without the project to the national per capita consumption level.

As Table 6 indicates, the larger the change induced by the project, the lower the weight. For example, with $\eta = 1$, if the beneficiaries are half as well off as the national average ($y = 0.5$), a 10 percent increase in their consumption level ($x = 0.1$) should be weighted by 1.91,[5] but a doubling of their consumption level ($x = 1.0$) should be weighted by 1.39. The weight falls by only 27 percent as x goes from 0.1 to 1.0. This is a rather moderate change, indicating that the errors in measuring x are not likely to be very serious. However, the rate of decline in the weights increases with more progressive weighting systems. For example, with $\eta = 2$, the weight is 3.64 when $x = 0.1$, but only 2.00 when $x = 1$; this is a 45 percent change.

Like other project data, the data on per capita consumption levels are never likely to be precise. Two types of approximations may need to be considered. First, the estimate of the "without project" income of the beneficiaries may be available as a range, say 50 to 70 percent of the national average level. A judgment will then be needed regarding the probability that this ratio will take a particular value—uniform (equal probability that $y = 0.5, 0.6,$ or 0.7), normal, lognormal, and so on. Second, if there are many beneficiaries within the range $0.5 < y < 0.7$, a judgment

5. If the change were marginal, the appropriate weight would be 2.0. A change of up to 20 percent might perhaps be regarded as marginal if $\eta = 1$.

Table 7. *Average and Midpoint Weights*

Income range	Average	Midpoint
$0.4 < y < 0.5$	2.23	2.22
$0.4 < y < 0.6$	2.02	2.00
$0.4 < y < 0.8$	1.71	1.67
$0.4 < y < 1.0$	1.48	1.43
$0.4 < y < 1.2$	1.30	1.25
$0.4 < y < 1.4$	1.16	1.11

will be needed regarding the distribution of the consumption increments within that group.

There are clearly many alternative ways of specifying the distribution of beneficiaries by income groups and the distribution of project benefits to each such group. Given judgments on these distributions, the relevant average weights can be readily calculated from a computer program. For example, if the distribution of beneficiaries by income is normal with a standard deviation of 20 percent within the specified range, and if project benefits are equally shared, the average weights, with $\eta = 1$, would be 1.37 if $0.5 < y < 1.0$, and 2.96 if $0.2 < y < 0.5$ (see the appendix to this chapter).

However, it may often be possible to use a much simpler procedure. Suppose, for example, that the consumption increments will accrue to a beneficiary group with $0.4 < y < 1.0$; that is, its income relative to the national average is somewhere between 40 percent and 100 percent. The average weight, as shown in Table 7, would then be 1.48, using the assumptions mentioned in the paragraph above. However, if one simply takes the midpoint ($y = 0.7$), the weight would be 1.43. Thus, even though the range $0.4 < y < 1.0$ is quite wide, the error made in using the midpoint weight is negligible. The same procedure may also be used for nonmarginal changes in consumption; that is, the nonmarginal weight relevant to the midpoint of the income range may be used as an approximation of the true weight.

A Summary of Adjustments Needed

Thus far, the discussion has focused only on the direct changes in consumption brought about by a project. But consumption changes may be induced in other ways. Once a consumption change has been identified, the same principles apply in its social evaluation. Nonetheless, the types of adjustment needed in two different cases are summarized here. For simplicity, only the net benefits in a typical project year are considered. Social conversion factors are also discussed.

Case 1. Assume that the project will produce a traded good, whose border price is unaffected by the project, with an incremental value of Rs X in border prices. For inputs, assume that Rs M is the cost in border prices of traded inputs, and Rs N is the cost in domestic prices of nontraded inputs. Then the net benefits of the project in efficiency prices is $E = (X - M) - (cN)$, where c is the conversion factor for revaluing domestic costs (N) in terms of border prices (as in Chapter 4).

Three types of adjustments may be necessary in recalculating the net benefits in social prices.

First, the actual payments to various inputs may exceed their alternative earnings elsewhere in the economy. This may happen not only in the case of labor, but also in the case of other inputs. The social cost of the incremental consumption expenditures owing to such "excess payments" may be separately calculated, along the lines discussed earlier, as

$$\sum_i C_i[\beta_i - (d_i/v)] = S_1.$$

Second, if the project is in the private sector, the incremental financial income will lead to additional private consumption expenditures, as in the example given earlier, and the net social cost of this consumption, $\sum_i C_i[\beta_i - (d_i/v)] = S_2$, should be subtracted from the efficiency benefits. Changes in public sector income because of taxes and subsidies need not be separately adjusted, since such income has a weight of unity by choice of unit of account. Similarly, private saving need not be separately treated if it is treated as equivalent to public sector income.

Third, if the project output were a nontraded good, with its price unaffected by the project, additional adjustments may be necessary. The gross benefits, Rs X, would in that case equal αR, where R is the incremental sales revenues in domestic prices, and α is the conversion factor that converts those revenues into border prices. For example, if the output is a consumption good, then Rs R represents the expenditures on competing consumption goods that are diverted to the project output, and αR is the resources, valued in border prices, released as a result of that diversion. The factor α would then be the consumption conversion factor (CCF). However, the diversion of expenditures to the project output from competing goods may change the income levels of those who supply the competing goods, thus giving rise to (positive or negative) leakages in consumption, S_3.

To summarize, the social net benefits can be written as

$$E = \text{efficiency net benefits} = \alpha R - M - cN$$

$$S = \text{social net benefits} = E - S_1 - S_2 + S_3,$$

where $S_1 = $ net social cost of consumption out of incremental income accruing to private suppliers of inputs, $S_2 = $ net social cost of consumption out of incremental income accruing directly to private producers and shareholders, and S_3 = net social cost of consumption avoided owing to changes in the expenditure patterns of users of the project output. This last term enters with a positive sign since reductions in expenditures elsewhere will reduce consumption, thereby saving β and losing d/v per unit of consumption affected.

The term S_3 is generally disregarded in practice, although it can, in principle, be significant. The term S_1 is also often regarded as negligible, except insofar as it relates to consumption out of incremental wage income. The most important term in projects involving private producers is S_2, which represents the cost of consumption out of additional farm incomes (as in irrigation projects) or out of additional profits and dividends (as in private industrial projects).

Case 2. Now consider the case in which the price of the project output (nontraded) falls in relation to what it would have been in the absence of the project. The price fall will create a "consumer surplus" gain, defined as $\Delta pQ + (\Delta p\Delta Q)/2$, where Δp and ΔQ are the changes in price and quantity, respectively, and Q is the "without project" quantity. If the project output were a final consumption good, this would represent a change in welfare directly perceived by the consumers. If the output were an intermediate good, the surplus would represent profits realized by the user industries. With reference to Figure 3 in Chapter 4, the evaluation of the price change will now proceed as follows.

In terms of efficiency analysis, and using domestic prices, the net benefits can be written as

$$N_1 = A + B + R - K - A = B + R - K,$$

where K is the economic costs adjusted by using shadow exchange rates (when relevant). The term A cancels out; although it is a benefit to the users, it is also a loss to producers who now receive a lower price on their "without project" production, Q. In terms of conversion factors, this may be rewritten as

$$N_2 = \beta B + rR - K',$$

where r is a demand-price conversion factor relevant to the expenditures diverted to the project output from other users (R), K' represents cost (using conversion factor adjustments) and β is a consumption conversion factor.

If the production is in the public sector and if the project outputs are consumption goods, then the social benefits can be written as:

$$N_3 = \frac{d}{v}(A + B) - \beta A + rR - K',$$

where the first term represents the welfare gain of the consumers, and βA represents the resource costs, in border prices, of the expenditures of the consumers financed out of the income gain (A). By rearranging terms, this can also be expressed as

$$N_3 = A\left(\frac{d}{v} - \beta\right) + \frac{d}{v}B + rR - K'.$$

The first term is the net social benefit of the "transfer" of A from the public sector to consumers. This assumes that all of the income gain (A) is consumed. If a part is saved, and if the savings are equally as valuable as public income, then the term A will be smaller since it will refer only to consumption changes.

If the project outputs are inputs into various industries, and if the gains to those industries are all saved and reinvested, and if the value of the savings equals that of public income, then the social benefits reduce to

$$N_4 = eB + rR - K',$$

where e is the conversion factor appropriate for adjusting the profits that those industries make on the incremental project output.

This analysis has assumed that all production is in the public sector. Thus, the loss of producer surplus on intramarginal production has been valued as βA. But the intramarginal production, as also the project production, may be in the private sector. The increased profits to those who participate in the project will lead to additional consumption, the net social cost of which must be deducted from the benefits. The losses on intramarginal production will lead to reduced consumption. The net social cost of this change in consumption will now need to be added to project benefits. Thus, the expression would now be

$$N_5 = N_3 + D_1\left(\beta - \frac{d}{v}\right) - D_2\left(\beta - \frac{d}{v}\right),$$

where D_1 is the change in consumption owing to the losses on intramarginal production, and D_2 is the gain in consumption owing to profits on project production. Note that if the competing producers are very poor—that is, $\beta - (d/v)$ is negative and large—the social losses on intramarginal production can be large enough to make the project unacceptable.

The switching of expenditures to project output may, of course, have price effects—whether or not the project affects its output prices. The resultant consumer and producer surpluses will then have to be evaluated similarly. The increased production of rice may lower the price of wheat, or a new railway link may lower the congestion costs on highways. The net social effects of such associated changes can significantly bear on a project's merit.

Social conversion factors

The expression used in Case I,

$$S = E - S_1 - S_2 + S_3,$$

with $$E = \alpha R - M - cN,$$

can be rewritten as

$$S = \alpha^* R - M - c^* N - S_2,$$

where $$\alpha^* R \equiv \alpha R + S_3 \text{ or } \alpha^* \equiv (\alpha R + S_3)/R,$$

and $$c^* N \equiv cN + S_1 \text{ or } c^* \equiv (cN + S_1)/N.$$

The new conversion factors, α^* and c^*, include the net social cost of consumption arising from expenditures on project outputs and project inputs. Such conversion factors are sometimes called social conversion factors. All such factors are ratios of the form $(E + S)/M$, where E is the efficiency cost, S is the net social cost of consumption, and M is the cost in market prices.[6] These factors are also called "extended efficiency" factors when all the d values equal unity.

One can therefore use either efficiency conversion factors (as explained in Chapter 4) with separate adjustments for consumption costs, or social conversion factors which combine the two effects. The use of social conversion factors is not uncommon in the applications of variable-weights approaches. In practice, however, it is much more convenient to use efficiency conversion factors and adjust for consumption leakages separately when necessary. The main reason is that the social conversion factors will change not only when the efficiency factors change, but also when the d values and v change over time, as they might.[7]

Sensitivity Tests

Shadow prices should obviously be included in the group of key parameters in sensitivity tests of NPVs and ERRs. Such tests or an alternative, risk analysis, are an integral part of good project analysis.

When only the investment premium is used, it is natural to use the parameter v in the sensitivity tests. Since this parameter operates only on the net social value of the consumption gains, its "cross-over" value needs to be defined with care. Focusing on only the consumption term, one can define v^* as the cross-over value for that term only. Thus,

$$\text{NPV}(C) \gtreqless 0 \quad \text{when} \quad v \lesseqgtr v^*,$$

where $$\text{NPV}(C) \equiv \sum_{t=0}^{T} \frac{1}{(1 + i)^t} \left[C_t \left(\frac{1}{v} - \beta_t \right) \right].$$

---

6. Detailed formulas for social conversion factors are given in Squire and van der Tak (1975), pp. 142–45.

7. The semi-input-output method discussed in Chapter 4, can be and has been used to generate sets of mutually consistent values of social factors. For that purpose, the d values and v are kept constant, as otherwise the analysis becomes too complex.

As $v \to \infty$,

$$\text{NPV}(C) \to - \sum_{t=0}^{T} [\beta_t C_t/(1 + i)^t],$$

and as $v \to 0$, $\text{NPV}(C) \to \infty$. Note that v can take negative values (if, for example, q is negative), although this is not realistic. It can also be zero, but in that case the investment numeraire cannot be used.

The relevant issue is whether the variations in the consumption term can alter the sign of the total NPV. As $v \to \infty$, one obtains the minimum possible value of the total NPV as

$$\min \text{NPV} = \text{NPV}(E) - \sum_{t=0}^{T} [\beta_t C_t/(1 + i)^t].$$

But min NPV can clearly be positive. In cases in which min NPV ≤ 0, one can define a cross-over value of v in the usual sense—that is, the value of v at which the project's NPV is zero—but when min NPV > 0 no cross-over value exists.

For all practical purposes, one can fix the range of v as 0.8–5. Consequently, if NPV $(v = 5) > 0$, one can be quite confident that the savings consideration does not matter. If the NPV is nonnegative only when $v < 0.8$, however, a fairly strong case for rejecting the project will emerge.

This form of analysis ignores the possible interdependence of v with other parameters, but it can be undertaken as a first step. It can be correct only when the rate of change of v is independent of its initial value. In fact, in the formulation above, it has been assumed that v is a constant over time. In that case, alternative initial values of v can only correspond to alternative values of the efficiency yield, q, or of the aggregate reinvestment propensity, s (see equations 5.3b and 5.3c in the summary of formulas in Chapter 5). Alternative initial values of v may also result from alternative assumptions about the pure rate of time preference. But if the latter is changed, the discount rate ARI ($=$ CRI in this case) will also change and the form of analysis illustrated above will be invalid, since the present value of all terms will be affected.

It may not, of course, be reasonable to assume constancy of v. If v falls, one can still experiment with alternative initial values of v without changing the ARI if one is prepared to be flexible regarding the date, T, at which v will converge to its neutral value (see equation 5.3a, Chapter 5). But then again, the alternative values of v must be interpreted as alternative values of q or s. The range of v should be determined accordingly.

Similar issues arise with variable weights. Since the elasticity parameter, η, is nonnegative, the project's NPV will be a minimum (maximum) when $\eta = 0$ if the beneficiaries are below (above) the CCL. The minimum value may still be positive, and the maximum value may still be negative. Thus, a cross-over value of η may not exist for the project's NPV, although it will always exist for the consumption term.

But η can be changed without altering the other parameters, such as v, only if the CRI is kept constant by changing the time preference rate, ρ, correspondingly[8] (see equation 5.4a, Chapter 5). If, however, ρ was disregarded in the derivation of the shadow prices in the first place, on the grounds that a positive value for this parameter cannot be easily rationalized, then CRI can be kept constant only by varying the expected rate of growth of per capita income.

The discount rate is another parameter commonly used in sensitivity tests. Once again, the interdependence issue arises. For example, if v is estimated from its rate of change and T, a change in ARI will change v unless the CRI is changed simultaneously. But if the ARI is to change while v is constant, other parameters, such as q, must also be changed.

The important point is that sensitivity tests should be constructed in a manner consistent with the system of equations used in estimating the various parameters, and a distinction should be made between usual parameters (such as q and s) and subjective parameters (η and ρ). The special assumptions required to change n, v, and the ARI independently in sensitivity tests should be consistent with the approach used in the first place.

Therefore, for the purposes of sensitivity analysis, either project analysts must be provided with a fairly wide range of mutually consistent parameters that apply to the country, or they should be familiar with the system of equations used so that they can themselves compute the mutually consistent sets needed. As a result, the simplicity of the traditional approach, in which the values of η and v are kept fixed (at $\eta = 0$ and $v = 1/\beta$), is reduced.

Appendix. Distribution Weights

Variable weights are most commonly specified in the constant-elasticity form discussed earlier,

$$d_i = (\bar{C}/C_i)^{\eta},$$

where $\bar{C}$ = per capita consumption level, C_i = per capita consumption level of group i, and η = the elasticity parameter.

Since this is a one-parameter (η) system, it offers considerable advantages in practice. A wide range of weighting schedules can be obtained by simply

8. This is not strictly true. As seen in Chapter 5, both the ARI and v depend on η directly, since they depend on how the benefits of public expenditures are distributed. It is usually assumed, for simplicity, that the net distributional effect of marginal public investments is zero, and only in that case can the η parameter be ignored in estimating the ARI and v.

Table 8. *d Values for Marginal Changes*

Relative consumption level ($\bar{C}/C$)	η				
	0	*0.5*	*1.0*	*1.5*	*2.0*
10.00	1.00	3.16	10.00	31.62	100.00
4.00	1.00	2.00	4.00	8.00	16.00
2.00	1.00	1.41	2.00	2.83	4.00
1.33	1.00	1.15	1.33	1.53	1.77
1.00	1.00	1.00	1.00	1.00	1.00
0.66	1.00	0.81	0.66	0.54	0.44
0.33	1.00	0.57	0.33	0.19	0.11
0.17	1.00	0.41	0.17	0.07	0.03
0.10	1.00	0.32	0.10	0.03	0.01

Source: Squire and van der Tak (1975), p. 64.

varying η, with $\eta = 0$ yielding the traditional constant-weight form. The weights referred to below are all based on this formula, since little may be gained by introducing more complex multiparameter systems.[9]

Marginal changes

For small changes from the consumption levels which would prevail without the project, the d values can be easily calculated by hand. Nonetheless, some illustrative values are shown in Table 8, with $\bar{C}$ as the national per capita level.

Nonmarginal changes

The marginal approach gives the same weight to all additional income received by any group, irrespective of how much the extra income is. If the value of income declines as income increases, however, successive parts of a large increment must have declining values. In that case, the marginal approach is not applicable.

For nonmarginal changes in consumption, d is defined as

$$d = \frac{\bar{C}(C_2^{1-\eta} - C_1^{1-\eta})}{(1-\eta)(C_2 - C_1)}, \qquad \text{for } \eta = 1$$

and

$$d = \frac{\bar{C}(\log C_2 - \log C_1)}{(C_1 - C_2)}, \qquad \text{for } \eta = 1$$

---

9. This appendix was prepared with the help of Pasquale Scandizzo.

Table 9. Nonmarginal Weights ($\eta = 1$)

y parameter	x parameter																			
	0.10	0.20	0.30	0.40	0.50	0.60	0.70	0.80	0.90	1.00	1.10	1.20	1.30	1.40	1.50	1.60	1.70	1.80	1.90	2.00
0.20	4.77	4.56	4.37	4.21	4.05	3.92	3.79	3.67	3.57	3.47	3.37	3.29	3.20	3.13	3.05	2.99	2.92	2.86	2.80	2.75
0.30	3.18	3.04	2.92	2.80	2.70	2.61	2.53	2.45	2.38	2.31	2.25	2.19	2.14	2.08	2.04	1.99	1.95	1.91	1.87	1.83
0.40	2.38	2.28	2.19	2.10	2.03	1.96	1.90	1.84	1.78	1.73	1.69	1.64	1.60	1.56	1.53	1.49	1.46	1.43	1.40	1.37
0.50	1.91	1.82	1.75	1.68	1.62	1.57	1.52	1.47	1.43	1.39	1.35	1.31	1.28	1.25	1.22	1.19	1.17	1.14	1.12	1.10
0.60	1.59	1.52	1.46	1.40	1.35	1.31	1.26	1.22	1.19	1.16	1.12	1.10	1.07	1.04	1.02	1.00	0.97	0.95	0.93	0.92
0.70	1.36	1.30	1.25	1.20	1.16	1.12	1.08	1.05	1.02	0.99	0.96	0.94	0.92	0.89	0.87	0.85	0.83	0.82	0.80	0.78
0.80	1.19	1.14	1.09	1.05	1.01	0.98	0.95	0.92	0.89	0.87	0.84	0.82	0.80	0.78	0.76	0.75	0.73	0.72	0.70	0.69
0.90	1.08	1.01	0.97	0.93	0.90	0.87	0.84	0.82	0.80	0.77	0.75	0.73	0.71	0.69	0.68	0.66	0.65	0.64	0.62	0.61
1.00	0.95	0.91	0.87	0.84	0.81	0.78	0.76	0.73	0.71	0.69	0.67	0.66	0.64	0.63	0.61	0.60	0.58	0.57	0.56	0.55
1.10	0.87	0.83	0.80	0.76	0.74	0.71	0.69	0.67	0.65	0.63	0.61	0.60	0.58	0.57	0.56	0.54	0.53	0.52	0.51	0.50
1.20	0.79	0.76	0.73	0.70	0.68	0.65	0.63	0.61	0.59	0.58	0.56	0.55	0.53	0.52	0.51	0.50	0.49	0.48	0.47	0.46
1.30	0.73	0.70	0.67	0.65	0.62	0.60	0.58	0.57	0.55	0.53	0.52	0.51	0.49	0.48	0.47	0.46	0.45	0.44	0.43	0.42
1.40	0.69	0.65	0.62	0.60	0.58	0.56	0.54	0.52	0.51	0.50	0.48	0.47	0.46	0.45	0.44	0.43	0.42	0.41	0.40	0.39
1.50	0.64	0.61	0.58	0.56	0.54	0.52	0.51	0.49	0.48	0.46	0.45	0.44	0.43	0.42	0.41	0.40	0.39	0.38	0.37	0.37
1.60	0.60	0.57	0.55	0.51	0.51	0.49	0.47	0.46	0.45	0.43	0.42	0.41	0.40	0.39	0.38	0.37	0.37	0.36	0.35	0.34
1.70	0.56	0.54	0.51	0.49	0.48	0.46	0.45	0.43	0.42	0.41	0.40	0.39	0.38	0.37	0.36	0.35	0.34	0.34	0.33	0.32
1.80	0.53	0.51	0.49	0.47	0.45	0.44	0.42	0.41	0.40	0.39	0.37	0.37	0.36	0.35	0.34	0.33	0.32	0.32	0.31	0.31
1.90	0.50	0.48	0.46	0.44	0.43	0.41	0.40	0.39	0.38	0.36	0.35	0.35	0.34	0.33	0.32	0.31	0.31	0.30	0.29	0.29
2.00	0.48	0.46	0.44	0.42	0.41	0.39	0.38	0.37	0.36	0.35	0.34	0.33	0.32	0.31	0.31	0.30	0.29	0.29	0.28	0.27

Note: $x = (C_2 - C_1)/C_1$, $y = C_1/\bar{C}$, where C_2 and C_1 are, respectively, "with project" and "without project" consumption levels, and $\bar{C}$ is the average national consumption level.

Table 10. Nonmarginal Weights ($\eta = 2$)

y parameter	\multicolumn{20}{c}{x parameter}

y parameter	0.10	0.20	0.30	0.40	0.50	0.60	0.70	0.80	0.90	1.00	1.10	1.20	1.30	1.40	1.50	1.60	1.70	1.80	1.90	2.00
0.20	22.73	20.83	19.23	17.86	16.67	15.63	14.71	13.89	13.16	12.50	11.90	11.36	10.87	10.42	10.00	9.26	9.26	8.93	8.62	8.33
0.30	10.10	9.26	8.59	7.94	7.41	6.94	6.54	6.17	5.85	5.56	5.29	5.05	4.83	4.63	4.44	4.27	4.12	3.97	3.83	3.70
0.40	5.68	5.21	4.81	4.46	4.17	3.91	3.68	3.47	3.29	3.13	2.98	2.84	2.72	2.60	2.50	2.40	2.31	2.23	2.16	2.08
0.50	3.64	3.33	3.08	2.88	2.57	2.50	2.35	2.22	2.11	2.00	1.90	1.82	1.74	1.47	1.60	1.54	1.48	1.43	1.38	1.33
0.60	2.53	2.31	2.14	1.98	1.85	1.74	1.63	1.54	1.46	1.39	1.32	1.26	1.21	1.16	1.11	1.07	1.03	0.99	0.96	0.93
0.70	1.86	1.70	1.57	1.46	1.36	1.28	1.20	1.13	1.07	1.02	0.97	0.93	0.89	0.85	0.82	0.78	0.76	0.73	0.70	0.68
0.80	1.42	1.30	1.20	1.12	1.04	0.98	0.92	0.87	0.82	0.78	0.74	0.71	0.68	0.65	0.63	0.60	0.58	0.56	0.54	0.52
0.90	1.12	1.03	0.95	0.88	0.82	0.77	0.73	0.69	0.65	0.62	0.59	0.56	0.54	0.51	0.49	0.47	0.46	0.44	0.43	0.41
1.00	0.91	0.83	0.77	0.71	0.67	0.63	0.59	0.56	0.53	0.50	0.48	0.45	0.43	0.42	0.40	0.38	0.37	0.36	0.34	0.33
1.10	0.75	0.69	0.64	0.59	0.55	0.52	0.49	0.46	0.43	0.41	0.39	0.38	0.36	0.34	0.33	0.32	0.31	0.30	0.28	0.26
1.20	0.63	0.56	0.53	0.50	0.46	0.43	0.41	0.39	0.37	0.35	0.33	0.32	0.30	0.29	0.28	0.27	0.26	0.25	0.24	0.23
1.30	0.54	0.49	0.46	0.42	0.39	0.37	0.35	0.33	0.31	0.30	0.28	0.27	0.26	0.25	0.24	0.23	0.22	0.21	0.20	0.20
1.40	0.46	0.43	0.39	0.36	0.34	0.32	0.30	0.28	0.27	0.26	0.24	0.23	0.22	0.21	0.20	0.20	0.19	0.18	0.18	0.17
1.50	0.40	0.37	0.34	0.32	0.30	0.28	0.26	0.25	0.23	0.22	0.21	0.20	0.19	0.19	0.18	0.17	0.16	0.16	0.15	0.15
1.60	0.36	0.33	0.30	0.28	0.26	0.24	0.23	0.22	0.21	0.20	0.19	0.18	0.17	0.16	0.16	0.15	0.14	0.14	0.13	0.13
1.70	0.31	0.29	0.27	0.25	0.23	0.22	0.20	0.19	0.18	0.17	0.16	0.16	0.15	0.14	0.14	0.13	0.13	0.12	0.12	0.12
1.80	0.28	0.26	0.24	0.22	0.21	0.19	0.18	0.17	0.16	0.15	0.15	0.14	0.13	0.13	0.12	0.12	0.11	0.11	0.11	0.10
1.90	0.25	0.23	0.21	0.20	0.18	0.17	0.16	0.15	0.15	0.14	0.13	0.13	0.12	0.12	0.11	0.11	0.10	0.10	0.10	0.09
2.00	0.23	0.21	0.19	0.18	0.17	0.16	0.14	0.14	0.14	0.13	0.12	0.11	0.11	0.10	0.10	0.10	0.09	0.09	0.09	0.08

Note: $x = (C_2 - C_1)/C_1$, $y = C_1/\bar{C}$, where C_2 and C_1 are, respectively, "with project" and "without project" consumption levels, and $\bar{C}$ is the average national consumption level.

Table 11. Nonmarginal Weights ($\eta = 3$)

y parameter	\\ x parameter → 0.10	0.20	0.30	0.40	0.50	0.60	0.70	0.80	0.90	1.00	1.10	1.20	1.30	1.40	1.50	1.60	1.70	1.80	1.90	2.00
0.20	108.47	95.49	85.06	76.53	69.44	63.48	58.39	54.01	50.21	46.88	43.93	41.32	38.99	36.89	35.00	33.28	31.72	30.29	28.98	27.76
0.30	32.14	28.29	25.20	22.68	20.58	18.81	17.30	16.40	14.88	13.89	13.02	12.24	11.55	10.95	10.37	9.66	9.40	8.98	8.59	8.23
0.40	13.56	11.94	10.63	9.57	8.68	7.93	7.30	6.75	6.28	5.86	5.49	5.17	4.87	4.61	4.38	4.16	3.97	3.79	3.62	3.47
0.50	6.94	6.11	5.44	4.98	4.44	4.06	3.74	3.46	3.21	3.00	2.81	2.64	2.50	2.36	2.24	2.13	2.03	1.94	1.85	1.78
0.60	4.02	3.54	3.15	2.83	2.57	2.35	2.15	2.00	1.80	1.74	1.63	1.53	1.44	1.37	1.30	1.23	1.17	1.12	1.07	1.03
0.70	2.53	2.23	1.95	1.76	1.62	1.45	1.36	1.25	1.17	1.09	1.02	0.96	0.91	0.86	0.82	0.78	0.74	0.71	0.68	0.65
0.80	1.69	1.49	1.33	1.20	1.09	0.99	0.91	0.84	0.78	0.73	0.69	0.65	0.61	0.58	0.55	0.52	0.50	0.47	0.45	0.43
0.90	1.19	1.05	0.93	0.84	0.76	0.70	0.62	0.59	0.55	0.51	0.48	0.45	0.43	0.40	0.38	0.37	0.35	0.33	0.32	0.30
1.00	0.87	0.76	0.68	0.61	0.56	0.51	0.47	0.43	0.40	0.38	0.35	0.33	0.31	0.30	0.28	0.27	0.25	0.24	0.23	0.22
1.10	0.65	0.57	0.51	0.46	0.42	0.38	0.35	0.32	0.30	0.28	0.26	0.25	0.23	0.22	0.21	0.20	0.19	0.18	0.17	0.17
1.20	0.50	0.44	0.39	0.35	0.32	0.29	0.27	0.25	0.23	0.22	0.20	0.19	0.18	0.17	0.16	0.15	0.15	0.14	0.13	0.13
1.30	0.39	0.35	0.31	0.28	0.25	0.23	0.21	0.20	0.18	0.17	0.16	0.15	0.14	0.13	0.13	0.12	0.12	0.11	0.11	0.10
1.40	0.32	0.28	0.25	0.22	0.20	0.19	0.17	0.16	0.15	0.14	0.13	0.12	0.11	0.11	0.10	0.10	0.09	0.09	0.08	0.08
1.50	0.26	0.23	0.20	0.18	0.16	0.15	0.14	0.13	0.12	0.11	0.10	0.10	0.09	0.09	0.08	0.08	0.08	0.07	0.07	0.07
1.60	0.21	0.19	0.17	0.15	0.14	0.12	0.11	0.11	0.10	0.09	0.09	0.08	0.08	0.08	0.08	0.08	0.08	0.07	0.07	0.07
1.70	0.18	0.16	0.14	0.12	0.11	0.10	0.10	0.09	0.08	0.08	0.07	0.07	0.06	0.07	0.07	0.07	0.06	0.06	0.06	0.05
1.80	0.15	0.13	0.12	0.10	0.10	0.09	0.08	0.07	0.07	0.06	0.06	0.06	0.05	0.06	0.06	0.05	0.05	0.05	0.05	0.05
1.90	0.13	0.11	0.10	0.09	0.08	0.07	0.07	0.06	0.06	0.05	0.05	0.05	0.05	0.05	0.05	0.05	0.04	0.04	0.04	0.04
2.00	0.11	0.10	0.09	0.08	0.07	0.06	0.06	0.05	0.05	0.05	0.04	0.04	0.04	0.04	0.04	0.04	0.04	0.04	0.03	0.03

Note: $x = (C_2 - C_1)/C_1$, $y = C_1/\bar{C}$, where C_2 and C_1 are, respectively, "with project" and "without project" consumption levels, and $\bar{C}$ is the average national consumption level.

where C_1 is the "without project" level and C_2 is the "with project" level (Squire and van der Tak, 1975, pp. 65, 66, and 136–37).

Tables 9, 10, and 11 show the weights relevant when the consumption increments are large. The variable x (column headings) is the change in consumption, or

$$x = \frac{C_2 - C_1}{C_1}.$$

The variable y (rows) is $y = C_1/\bar{C}$, that is, the relative income status of the beneficiaries without the project. Assume that, in a particular project year, the level of consumption of the beneficiaries without the project would be 50 percent of the national average level ($y = 0.5$). Assume also that the consumption level doubles as a result of the project ($x = 1.0$). If $\eta = 1$ (Table 9), the relevant weight is 1.39, much less than the marginal weight of 2. If $\eta = 2$, the correct weight is 2, as compared with the marginal weight of 4, so that the error involved in using marginal weights increases with the progressivity of the system.

Another feature is that the larger the consumption increment, the lower the weight. Thus, with $\eta = 1$ and $y = 0.5$, if consumption with the project is three times higher ($x = 2$), the weight is 1.10, not 1.39. The corresponding number with $\eta = 2$ is 1.33, not 2.00. The rate of decline increases with η. The use of nonmarginal weights may be recommended whenever the consumption increment is 20 percent or more relative to the "without project" consumption level, assuming $\eta = 1$.

Averaging over ranges

There is bound to be considerable uncertainty, in practice, regarding the income status of the beneficiaries. For example, even if it is felt that all beneficiaries have the same "without project" income, only an estimate of the range of that income level may be possible. The average distribution weight $(\bar{d})$ over this range would be

$$\bar{d} = \sum_i p_i d_i, \quad \sum p_i = 1,$$

where p_i is the probability that the income level is i.

If the distribution is uniform, with $p_i = p_j$, this simplifies to $\bar{d} = p \sum d_i$. This can be readily calculated by hand. For example, if $C/\bar{C}$ could be 0.5, 0.6, 0.7, or 0.8, with equal probability, then the average weight would be 1.59 (with $\eta = 1$).

One would obtain the same result if it were assumed that there were four income groups affected, with weights of 2.00, 1.67, 1.43, and 1.25, sharing equally in the project benefits. There are clearly many ways, however, in which the variation of income among the beneficiaries and the distribution

Table 12. *Weights for Income Ranges*

Range of y^a	$\eta = 1$	$\eta = 2$
$0.2 < y < 0.5$	2.96	9.10
$0.5 < y < 1.0$	1.37	1.93
$0.5 < y < 1.5$	1.04	1.13
$0.9 < y < 2.0$	0.71	0.52

a. $y = C_1/\bar{C}$, where C_1 is "without project" consumption, and $\bar{C}$ is the national per capita level.

of project benefits can be specified. A computer program will be needed to derive the relevant weights for broad ranges of income under various assumptions regarding the nature of the data.

For example, the weights shown in Table 12 were computed assuming that the distribution of beneficiaries by income is normal, with a standard deviation of 20 percent within the specified range. If the weights are specified in this way, the project analyst need only estimate the range within which the project benefits are likely to accrue. Fairly broad ranges may be sufficient; for example, they may be set to correspond to the quintiles of the national income distribution scale.

CHAPTER 7

Using Variable Weights: Implications

THE IMPLICATIONS OF USING variable weights in practice differ from case to case. It is possible, nonetheless, to bring out the general nature of these implications in broad terms. The first section comments briefly on selected issues of project design and selection. The final section brings out the implications for pricing and cost recovery policies, which are often integral parts of project work.

Project Choices

As discussed in the previous chapter, with the new method a project's net present value (NPV) can be conveniently decomposed into two parts: first, the NPV of the project using the traditional methodology (but using the ARI as the discount rate) and second, the NPV of the consumption changes induced by the project. This implies that the evaluation of a project cannot be done unless it is feasible to use the traditional approach. In other words, if in a particular case it is not possible to measure a project's ERR in the usual sense, it is also not possible to measure the ERR in terms of the new method (the social rate of return, SRR). Moreover, the calculation of the traditional ERR is the best that one can do in cases in which the induced consumption effects of a project are unknown.

Projects in public utilities, for example, are among those which frequently present problems for economic analysis, even in the traditional sense. The main reason for this is that in many developing countries public utility services such as power, telecommunications, and potable water are rationed, the actual rates charged having little to do with market clearing. Economic analysis then requires an examination of the rationing rules employed, prices implicit in rationing, and the changes in the implicit prices brought about by an investment. Analyses of the pertinent markets are commonly not made in sufficient detail. Instead, the ERR is typically based on actual (or expected) tariff rates. A low ERR in that case does not necessarily indicate an unsound project, but rather an unsound pricing policy. If the economic analysis is restricted in this manner, a satisfactory social evaluation in terms of the new method cannot be made.

A somewhat different case occurs in general-purpose transport projects. The quantification of the traditional ERR may not present any special problems in such cases, but its extension to include consumption effects may. Consider, for example, a road project. The benefits of such a project can be measured as the "consumer surplus" under the transport demand function or, equivalently, as the net gain of the benefits and losses that accrue to the transport industry and to the users of transport. The logical equivalence is discussed in Harberger (1976, Chap. 10) and van der Tak and Ray (1971). Practical approaches that use the same methodology but focus on the direct evaluation of producer and consumer benefits are discussed in Beenhakker (1979) and Carnemark, Biderman, and Bovet (1976).

Direct evaluation of the benefits and costs to consumers and producers is, however, only feasible for roads that service readily identifiable users. In most cases, the transport demand function has to be used. But since the surplus under the demand curve is the net effect of many gains and losses, the relevant weights cannot be determined unless very special assumptions are made.[1] Thus, even if the traditional calculation of the ERR is possible, the SRR calculation may be rather problematic.

Although these types of problems may arise in all sectors, the scope for applying the new approach is typically quite wide. The implications of applying it will depend on whether differential distribution weights are used. If only the investment premium is used, then the main effects will be:

- The economic rate of return will always be equal to or less than the traditional rate of return, assuming that the investment numeraire is chosen. This does not mean that it will be harder to justify projects, since the discount rate will also tend to be lower. The composition of projects will change, however. Other things being equal, projects which lead to greater public sector revenues or private reinvestments will be favored. The public sector investment program will tend to be more oriented toward relatively capital-intensive infrastructure projects because they contribute relatively more to savings than do projects that directly increase private sector incomes. For example, a steel project with an 8 percent traditional rate of return will also have an 8 percent rate of return in terms of the new approach, if project surpluses accrue in the form of savings. Yet it will now appear more attractive if the discount rate, ARI, is lower, as it is likely to be.
- The techniques of production chosen will also be more capital-intensive than otherwise whenever projects involve higher payments to labor than they would otherwise have received. This is because in such cases the new shadow wage rate will tend to be higher than the

1. For example, if the benefits can be assumed to be distributed in proportion to the distribution of income in the country, the special weight "D," suggested in Squire and van der Tak (1975, pp. 66–67), can be used.

traditional shadow wage rate; indeed, the new shadow wage rate may be higher than even the market wage rate.

• Similarly, design changes or policies that increase a project's contribution to public or private savings will be more attractive. In particular, higher levels of cost recovery will be desirable. In regard to pricing policy, the optimal prices of inputs and outputs may be higher, but never less than the optimal prices in the traditional approach.

The implications of introducing differential consumption weights will depend on the weighting scheme chosen. If one uses the constant-elasticity form, the generalizations made above will remain broadly unchanged as long as the beneficiaries belong to income groups above the critical consumption level. In fact, the pro-growth bias of using an investment premium will be enhanced in that case, since the greater the progressivity of the distribution weights, the greater the net social cost of consumption of those above the critical level.

If, however, the beneficiaries are poor relative to the critical level and remain poor for the first ten years or so even after the project, the general implications will be reversed. Projects will be more consumption-oriented and labor-intensive. Cost recoveries will be low, and input and output prices may be higher or lower than their optimal levels would otherwise be.

The new approach may be especially useful when important tradeoffs arise concerning the selection of beneficiaries. The criteria for the selection of beneficiaries are very important for the development and design of many projects. Yet general exhortations to maximize the number of beneficiaries or to choose them from poverty groups may be misleading. Consider, for example, a land settlement project. One of the important issues in such a case concerns the optimal size of holding per settler family. Depending on the project circumstances and crops involved, a fairly wide range of sizes may be feasible, such as two to six hectares or eight to sixteen hectares. The smaller the size, the greater the number of beneficiaries that can be accommodated within a given project area. A small size is therefore often regarded as desirable from the social point of view, other things being equal.

For a given project area, the net present value of the project as traditionally calculated, N_1, will vary with the holding size per settler family. Its variation will depend on how returns to agricultural operations vary with size—whether or not there are economies of scale. It will also depend on how the costs of the associated physical and social infrastructure vary with the number of beneficiaries. Figure 5 depicts a possible outcome, with the optimal size being any size between eight and twelve hectares.

The weighted NPVs are shown as N_2 and N_3. If beneficiaries are "nonpoor" (above the critical consumption level, CCL), then the NPV will lie below N_1—the line N_3. Conversely, if beneficiaries are "poor" (below the CCL), the relevant line is N_2. This is based on the assumption that preproject income levels of the beneficiaries do not affect the NPV.

Figure 5. *Optimum Size of Holding*

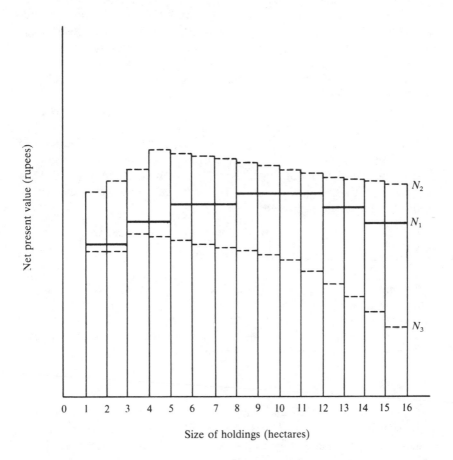

Size of holdings (hectares)

The proposition that the greater the number of beneficiaries the better the project, is taken by many as a truism. If one looks at N_1 and compares the five-hectare unit with the seven-hectare unit, a range over which the NPV does not change, the smaller size is just as good as the larger. Once progressive weights are used, the smaller size appears preferable—both N_2 and N_3 decline over that range. But comparing five hectares with nine hectares, one faces the tradeoff between slicing a bigger cake for fewer families with nine hectares each and slicing a smaller cake to more families with five hectares each. The better option depends on how fast the weights decline—the smaller unit size is better in Figure 5, but this need not be so in general.

The choice of income groups from which the beneficiaries are to be drawn may be an important issue in itself. If progressive weights are used, it is obvious that the poorer the beneficiaries the better the project, for any given size of holding, if all other things are equal.

It is possible, however, that the poorer the beneficiaries, the less their ability to perform. If so, the N_1 line corresponding to poor groups will lie below the N_1 line for the nonpoor groups. It is conceivable in such cases that the N_3 line shown in Figure 5 will lie above, not below, the N_2 line, or that they will cross. Judgments regarding the selection of beneficiaries will be sensitive both to productivity effects and to the progressivity of the distribution weights.

Tradeoffs of this type are among the issues examined for alternative farming systems for settlement projects in Kenya by MacArthur (1978). Similar tradeoffs arise frequently for other types of projects also. The size of the command areas of an irrigation scheme, the service standards and target groups for urban housing, the degree of farm mechanization, and so on, are questions better handled through the new approach when distributional concerns matter.[2]

Pricing and Cost Recovery Policies

Pricing and cost recovery issues are often integral parts of project economic work, either because they bear directly on a project's merit or because they are prominent in the sectoral context in which a project has to be seen. The implications of the variable-weights approach for pricing and cost recovery policies are discussed below.

Pricing Policy

There is by now a vast literature on pricing policy, covering not only general theory but also just about any special problem one cares to specify in any sector. It is well known that the old rule, "price should equal short-run marginal cost," is often far too simple because of many reasons, such as those relating to the variability of prices over time, investment policy, and the effect of prices on future demand and tastes.[3] A full-scale development of a new type of pricing policy is not attempted here. Instead, the discussion focuses only on the most elementary implications of using variable weights in this context. For this limited purpose, it will suffice to concentrate on the simple marginal cost pricing rule.

Suppose the problem at hand is to decide the optimal price (and hence the optimal output) of a nontraded product to be produced by a public sector

2. See Hughes (1976), Cleaver (1980), and Bruce and Kimaro (1978) for detailed analysis, respectively, of urban housing, farm mechanization issues, and irrigation.

3. For some excellent discussions of pricing policy in different sectors, see Bennathan and Walters (1979), Turvey and Anderson (1977), and Walters (1968). The determination of optimal prices depends on the investment policy being followed; this interrelationship is the key ingredient in the concept of the "long-run marginal cost."

project. Assuming that all relevant conversion factors are unity, the net benefits of the project, which is to be maximized, is

$$B = S + E - K,$$

where $S = $ consumer surplus, $E = $ expenditures on the product, and $K = $ costs. Writing the demand function as $p = f(q)$, it is easily seen that

$$B = \int_0^q f(q)\,dq - pq + pq - K$$

$$= \int_0^q f(q)\,dq - K$$

$$= [\text{willingness to pay}] - [\text{cost}].$$

At optimum output, $\partial B/\partial q = 0$. Thus, the old rule is obtained:

$$p = \frac{\partial K}{\partial q} = \text{marginal cost} = m.$$

Introducing conversion factors, using variable weights, and assuming a consumer good, one can write the maximand as

$$B = \sum_i \frac{d_i}{v} S_i + \sum_i \beta_i E_i - K - \sum_j \left(\beta_j - \frac{d_j}{v} \right) F_j,$$

where $\sum \beta_i E_i$ and K are expenditures and costs in border prices; β_i, β_j are consumption conversion factors; F_j are consumption changes owing to transfers associated with the use of inputs j; and S_i are consumer surpluses.

To illustrate the derivation of the optimal price with a minimum of clutter, assume a single consumer (suffix c) and a single input (suffix f), and a single consumption conversion factor β. Thus, at the optimal output,

$$\frac{d_c}{v} \frac{\partial S}{\partial q} + \beta \frac{\partial E}{\partial q} = \frac{\partial K}{\partial q} + \left(\beta - \frac{d_f}{v} \right) \frac{\partial F}{\partial q}$$

$$= m + r,$$

where $m = $ marginal production cost, valued in border prices, and $r = $ net social consumption cost of using the input. Noting that

$$\frac{\partial S}{\partial q} = - qf'(q),$$

and that $\partial E/\partial q = p + qf'(q) \equiv e$, one can write

$$m + r = \frac{d_c}{v}(p - e) + \beta e$$

$$= \beta p + \left(\beta - \frac{d_c}{v} \right) qf'(q)$$

$$= \beta p + z,$$

where $z \equiv (\beta - d_c/v)qf'(q)$. Thus, the optimal price is

$$p = \frac{m + r - z}{\beta}.$$

In the special case in which the factor owner, who receives the consumption transfer through employment, and the consumer are both at the critical consumption level, $r = z = 0$ and

$$p = \frac{m}{\beta}.$$

That is, the optimal price is the marginal cost in border prices times the inverse of the consumption conversion factor.[4]

In other words, the price of this commodity should not be set at its marginal cost, valued at border prices. An adjustment is necessary to reflect the fact that taxes and subsidies bear on other markets. If, on average, other commodities are subsidized, then $\beta > 1$ and $p < m$. Conversely, if taxes dominate, $\beta < 1$ and $p > m$.

It is possible, of course, that the product price has to be taken as a parameter by the project entity. In that case, the pricing problem disappears, but the optimal production level will still be affected by consumption transfers through employment. This, of course, is true if and only if additional employment necessarily involves consumption transfers.

Will the optimal price be higher or lower than the traditional price? Since $\beta p = m + r - z$,

$$\beta p \gtrless m \text{ as } r - z \gtrless 0.$$

The value of r is likely to be negative if the factor owners are poor (relative to the CCL). Given $\beta - (d_f/v) < 0$, the sign of r will depend on the sign of $\partial F/\partial q$. The latter will be positive if the amount of consumption transfers increases with employment. Other things being equal, poverty of the factor owners will then imply a lower price, and hence higher output and employment.

The term z will be positive if the consumers are poor (relative to the CCL) since $f'(q) < 0$. Thus, poverty of the consumers would also make the optimal price lower than it otherwise would be. This is the expected result.

Conversely, if both the consumers and the factor owners are nonpoor (relative to the CCL), $\beta p > m$. Nothing can be said in the intermediate cases where the factor owners and the consumers lie on different sides of the CCL.

---

4. If marginal production costs are expressed in terms of foreign currency units instead of in "border rupees," this rule can also be written as $p = (\text{SER})\bar{m}$, $\bar{m}$ being the marginal cost in foreign currency units. Note that the definition of the SER must correspond to whatever conversion factor is relevant. In the case being discussed, the appropriate definition is SER $= \text{OER}/\beta$, β being the consumption conversion factor, and OER the actual exchange rate.

But since the consumption gain of consumers is likely to be higher than that of factor owners, the income status of the former group might well dominate.

This discussion suggests that the traditional pricing doctrines will remain approximately correct if production processes are capital-intensive (assuming it is labor that receives excess payments), and if the gains to users of the products are largely reinvested (as might happen in the case of incremental profits of industrial users).

It is obvious that the new approach will bear heavily on such issues as "lifeline" rates for residential electric power (see Munasinghe and Warford, 1978) and cross-subsidization of poorer neighborhoods in other public utilities. The interesting issue would be whether the so-called poor users of electricity, potable water, telecommunications, urban transport, and the like, who typically receive subsidies, are indeed poor enough relative to the CCL. Since the latter may, in some cases, be even below the absolute poverty line (as discussed in Chapter 5), it is not clear at first sight whether the subsidization of such services will be at all warranted in terms of the new approach. At any rate, the new approach is likely to lead to more conservative attitudes to these issues, except insofar as subsidies can be administered in a highly discriminatory manner.

Cost Recovery Policy

Cost recovery issues are essentially pricing issues in another guise, although they have some distinguishing elements. To begin with, consider a traditional pricing policy, based on marginal costs, for a public enterprise. Such a policy may or may not be optimally based on short-run marginal costs, but that is not important to the arguments here.

Such a policy may well satisfy the financial requirements of revenue-generating public enterprises, however defined—whether in the form of a minimum return on net fixed assets, a norm for surplus cash generation, or some other form. In the event that it does not satisfy financial requirements, there are two possibilities. First, the financial standards that will be violated will affect the economic efficiency of the operations. For example, loss-making enterprises may become undisciplined and their X-efficiency may fall. Alternatively, an enterprise may lose the autonomy in decisionmaking required to carry out its annual operations and its investment programs efficiently. If economic and financial performance standards are interdependent in this sense, such conflicts cannot arise if the marginal-cost-based pricing policy is properly defined in the first place. Second, some financial standards may be imposed on the enterprise, even though they are not necessary to ensure the economic efficiency of its conduct. In that case, economic and financial standards will be mutually independent, and therefore genuine conflicts may arise.

The traditional approach to pricing policy leads to the conclusion that such independent financial norms should be avoided. Financial policy should accommodate economic policy, not replace it. Moreover, there should be no problems in avoiding such conflicts. If the marginal-cost-based pricing policy leads to recurrent losses, and if such losses do not affect economic performance, the losses can and should be made up by cash transfers from the central treasury. The traditional pricing theory implies a theory of the generation and allocation of funds within the public sector: that cash transfers can be made in indefinite amounts at negligible economic cost per unit of transfer. In effect, this implies that cash transfers can be financed by lump-sum taxation or almost lump-sum taxation. If this is not so—as implied by budgetary "tightness"—then the marginal cost per unit of transfer must be taken into account in defining the pricing policy in the first place. This marginal cost may increase as the amount of transfer increases.

Consider the case in which economies of scale or indivisibilities are so great that a marginal-cost-based pricing policy will lead to large financial losses or to low levels of cost recovery.[5] The traditional prescription in such cases is to introduce multipart tariffs designed to minimize the economic costs (or deadweight losses) per unit of revenues raised. But such a policy is desirable only if a financial constraint exists, independent or not. If transfers can be financed by lump-sum taxes, and if the receipt of subsidies does not affect economic efficiency, one should be indifferent to multipart tariffs. Such tariffs will be desirable only if the marginal economic cost per unit of transfer exceeds the marginal economic cost per unit of revenues raised through them.

Cost recovery issues are prominent in the case of irrigation projects, which often tend to have very low levels of cost recovery, at least when dams and major canals have to be constructed. It is, of course, seldom possible to price irrigation water directly because of various practical difficulties, but even if it were possible, a marginal-cost-based pricing policy need not do more than cover the annual costs of operation.[6]

It is common, therefore, to consider special benefit levies on farmers to recover costs. But it may be difficult to rationalize the imposition of benefit levies if general revenues can be raised at little cost. This is because benefit levies will almost always involve deadweight losses or excess burden through their effects on input mixes, crop choices, or labor supply.

---

5. Annual losses and low cost recoveries are different concepts. The former implies the latter, but not vice versa. Consider a road to serve a specific user, such as a mining company. A toll to cover marginal user costs may avoid annual cash outflows for maintenance, but will not recover the initial investment costs.

6. Quantity-rationing rules, which are easier to implement, are also indirect pricing rules. They may therefore be designed to simulate the effects of a marginal-cost-based pricing policy when direct pricing is infeasible. But even if such quantity-rationing rules could be designed, they would not, of course, generate any revenues.

The doctrine that "beneficiaries should pay" is commonly put forward in this context. In terms of the traditional framework, this is an extra-economic rule. It is also not helpful since the question arises as to how the beneficiaries should pay—through sales taxes on farm products, input taxes, or land taxes? Moreover, suppose that there are two mutually exclusive options, A and B. With A, the NPV of the irrigation project will be Rs50 million, and with B it will be Rs30 million. Suppose also that the imposition of benefit levies will be relatively much easier with A than with B, so that beneficiaries will pay much more with A than with B. Which should be chosen? How does one introduce the doctrine in analyzing tradeoffs? One cannot, in fact, do so without formally introducing a weight on public revenues.

Looking at the overall fiscal effects of an irrigation project also does not diffuse the issue. It is true that if one calculates the total increment in tax revenues that will occur directly or indirectly from an irrigation project and defines it as the "recovery," then cost recoveries will be high, perhaps even higher than 100 percent. But this may well be true of many projects in other sectors as well. The problem is that the normative significance of any particular level of cost recovery in that broad sense is unclear. If it is 50 percent in one case, should tax revenues then be increased and, if so, which taxes? If not, should a special penalty be charged against the project; if so, how much should that penalty be?

The difficulties of addressing these issues within the traditional framework also leads to other extra-economic prescriptions, such as "earmarking"—the idea that each sector should cover all the costs of projects within that sector. Thus, highway user charges should be set so as to cover the total investment and maintenance program for roads. All costs in the irrigation sector—or, more broadly, in the agricultural sector—should be covered from revenues generated within agriculture. But this line of thinking is contrary to any economic rationale. Taxation and pricing principles then become indeterminate and depend on how broadly or narrowly one defines the sector in which costs are to be recovered. Low procurement prices may then be justified for wheat in order to cover the costs of irrigating wheat crops—thereby destroying much of the benefits of the irrigation project. But such policies may not be needed if the entire agricultural sector is grouped together. In the case of roads, Walters (1968, p. 86) points out that "the more homogeneous the subset of roads for which a balanced budget is required, the greater the likelihood of inefficient pricing. It is easy to show that *a fortiori*, insistence on a budgetary equilibrium for a particular road may lead to quite appalling results."[7]

---

7. All this is obvious from the theory of optimum taxation. One can only lose by introducing a multiplicity of revenue constraints when a single constraint is appropriate. The links between optimum taxation theory, the discussion in this section, and shadow prices are very close. See Atkinson and Stiglitz (1980), especially Lectures 11, 12, 15, 16.

The analysis of cost recovery issues becomes easier with the variable-weights approach. It is seldom true that public funds can be expanded at will with negligible excess burden—even inflationary financing is not costless. Consequently, there is a strong case for introducing a positive marginal social cost per unit of transfer. In fact, the assumption that there is a strict constraint on expanding public revenues may be quite realistic in some developing countries, and, if so, it is the marginal social benefit of public expenditures that becomes relevant. In other words, the cost of transferring resources to a loss-making enterprise would then be the benefits from other expenditures forgone as a result. In either case, the parameter v should be introduced in the analysis, as discussed in Chapter 5.

To return to the issue of benefit levies in the case of irrigation projects, a benefit levy, say, a land tax, will be desirable if the beneficiaries are above the CCL, and undesirable otherwise. Thus, if Y is the increment in farm income, the net social cost of the consumption induced is MPC $Y[\beta - (d/v)]$ as before, MPC being the marginal propensity to consume. For nonpoor beneficiaries, this is positive, and a levy that reduces Y must also reduce the social cost. Moreover, since the possibility of benefit taxation arises only because of the project, the project can be credited with it. Thus, its weighted NPV will increase. This can be checked by increasing the direct charges on farmers assumed in the numerical examples given in Chapter 6 (Tables 1 and 5).

The upper limit to the levy is not, however, the net disposable income gain as conventionally measured, but a lower amount if an allowance for risk is made, such as the "certainty equivalent." This is often called "rent" in cost recovery literature (see Duane, 1975). But since it is hard to design lump-sum levies, the optimum levy is likely to be even less.

The key point is that the parameter v allows the general fiscal constraint to be brought into project considerations in a systematic way. The value of v, other things being equal, determines what the optimum value of the levy should be. Of course, it is not just the levy that is affected. As seen in the earlier section on pricing, all input and output prices will now be determined by equations of the type $p = (m + r - z)/\beta$. Thus, the general fiscal constraint will be reflected consistently throughout all project decisions.

Finally, one must refer to the important notion of "horizontal equity," the desirability of treating similar persons equally. This is of special importance for benefit levies in irrigation projects. The introduction of special levies in area A will violate this precept unless similar beneficiaries in other projects are subjected to levies along the same lines. This, in fact, is a common argument against introducing benefit levies piecemeal. Such cost recovery issues are, therefore, often thought to be sectorwide rather than project-specific concerns.

Notes on Shadow Wage Rates

THE VALUATION OF LABOR has long been a central part of cost-benefit literature. Yet, the recent surge of empirical research into labor markets has brought out the diversity of such markets and the complexity of validating hypotheses in this area. Many of the popular notions of the past, such as that of "surplus" labor, appear to have been nothing more than overly simplistic stylizations. The evaluation of labor costs in practice is therefore likely to require substantial work on the particular labor markets relevant to the project.

The first section of this appendix presents some formulations for the shadow wage rate based on an approach frequently used in the literature. Subsequent sections bring out some of the limitations of that approach. The issue of how leisure might be valued from the social point of view is also discussed. The final section comments more informally on some issues frequently encountered in practice.

Standard Formulations

Shadow wage rates are often derived from a "dual economy" model, for example, the model developed by Little and Mirrlees. Suppose investments occur only in the industrial, or the "modern," sector, at a fixed real wage (w), drawing labor from the agricultural, or "backward," sector. The withdrawn labor forgoes income equal to the average farm product (a), which now accrues to those left behind. At the same time, agricultural output falls by m, the marginal product, which is not offset by additional work by the remaining rural work force. Assuming that the industrial surplus accrues only to the public sector for reinvestment, the maximand, at any point in time, is the social value of national income, or

$$Q = LW(w) + L_r W(a) + \lambda[F(L, K) - wL],$$

where L is the industrial labor force, L_r is the rural labor force, and $L + L_r = N$, a constant. The industrial production function, with labor and capital, is $F(L, K)$, and λ is the utility value of additional investment. $W(\cdot)$ is the social valuation function; $W(\cdot) = \phi(U(\cdot)) = U(\cdot)$, assuming ϕ is utilitarian. The value of λ must be chosen correctly in each period so as to maximize the discounted present value of consumption over time.[1]

---

1. Full statements of the model and the necessary assumptions are available in several places, for example, Anand (1981), Lal (1980), Lal and Squire (1980), and Stern (1977b).

The shadow wage rate (SWR) for industrial labor is now obtained as SWR $= F_L$, by setting $\partial Q/\partial L = 0$. This is, using the investment numeraire,

$$\text{SWR} = w - \frac{1}{\lambda}[W(w) - W(a) + (a - m)W'(a)]. \tag{8.1}$$

For simplicity, all conversion factors are assumed to be unity. The value of investment in terms of consumption is now $s \equiv \lambda/W'$. With this definition, the above equation can be rewritten as

$$\text{SWR} = w - \frac{1}{s}\left[\frac{W(w) - W(a)}{W'(a)} + (a - m)\right]. \tag{8.2}$$

A number of simple results can be readily obtained from these two equations. Two cases are developed using only the shadow price of investments. Income distribution weights are introduced in the third case. The implications for efficiency pricing are also mentioned.

Case 1

Assume $W(C) = C$. The first term in parenthesis in (8.2) then becomes $(w - a)$, the urban-rural wage gap. The standard Little–Mirrlees definition of the SWR is now obtained as

$$\text{SWR} = w - \frac{1}{s}(w - m),$$

or

$$= m + (w - m)\left(1 - \frac{1}{s}\right) \tag{8.3}$$

$$= [\text{Marginal product forgone}] +$$
$$[\text{Net social cost of incremental}$$
$$\text{project-induced consumption}].$$

This formula is valid for more general $W(\cdot)$ functions if the change is small, since in that case $W(w) - W(a) = (w - a)W'(a)$.

This savings–corrected or extended efficiency SWR will be less than the wage rate, w, unless s tends to infinity. It will, however, be greater than the efficiency shadow wage rate (EWR), since, with $s = 1$, EWR $= m$. A value of $s = 2$ is not unlikely in practice. In that case the SWR will be the arithmetic average of the EWR and the project wage w.

Case 2

In order to introduce leisure in a systematic way, define $W(y, l) = U(y, l) = ky + g(l)$, with constant k. Measured consumption is y, and l is leisure. This definition assumes that the elasticity of substitution between

---

Anand's discussion is the most general one and summarizes, as well as extends, many of the theoretical results in this area.

income and leisure is infinity. This is one version of the "full income" concept.

The supply price of a migrant, $\hat{w}$, can now be defined as

$$U(\hat{w}, l_2) = U(a, l_1),$$

with $l_2 =$ leisure with the industrial job, and $l_1 =$ leisure on the farm. Presumably, $l_2 < l_1$, and therefore $\hat{w} > a$. Equilibrium requires

$$k\hat{w} + g(l_2) = ka + g(l_1).$$

This implies

$$[g(l_1) - g(l_2)]/k = \hat{w} - a. \tag{8.4}$$

Note that

$$\theta \equiv [g(l_1) - g(l_2)]/k[l_2 - l_1]$$

will approximate, for small changes, the marginal rate of substitution between income and leisure. Now $\theta(l_2 - l_1)$ is the value of the loss of leisure—that is, the cost of additional effort, f.

Using (8.2), (8.4), and noting that $W'(a) = k$, $W(w) - W(a) = W(w) - W(\hat{w}) = k(w - \hat{w})$, we have

$$\text{SWR} = w - \frac{1}{s}[(w - \hat{w}) + a - m] \tag{8.5}$$

or

$$\text{SWR} = w - \frac{1}{s}[(w - m) - f] \tag{8.6}$$

$$= m + (w - m)\left(1 - \frac{1}{s}\right) + \frac{f}{s}$$

$$= [\text{The SWR as in (8.3)}] +$$
$$[\text{The weighted cost of extra effort}].$$

Setting $s = 1$, the efficiency wage is simply

$$\text{EWR} = m + f. \tag{8.7}$$

If the migrant were completely idle on the farm, $\text{EWR} = f > 0$. Also, the savings-corrected shadow wage rate will be higher than the EWR, since

$$\text{SWR} = \text{EWR} + \left(1 - \frac{1}{s}\right)(w - m - f).$$

Case 3

I now introduce distribution weights on full income. Define

$$W(\cdot) = U(y, l) = \frac{1}{1 - \eta}(y^*)^{1 - \eta}, \quad \eta \neq 1$$

and

$$y^* = ky + g(l).$$

We now have

$$W'(a) = ka^{*-\eta}$$

and
$$W'(a)/\lambda = [W'(a)/W'(\bar{c})][W'(\bar{c})/\lambda]$$
$$= d_a^*/v,$$

with $\bar{c}$ as the average national consumption level, and v as the corresponding definition of the shadow price of investments (as in Squire–van der Tak, 1975). The weight on full income is

$$d_a^* = \left(\frac{a^*}{\bar{c}^*}\right)^{-\eta}.$$

Using these relations, we can write, for small changes,

$$\text{SWR} = w - \frac{d_a^*}{v}[(w-m)-f]. \tag{8.8}$$

This is only slightly different from Squire–van der Tak (1975, p. 83, equation 16). We also have not allowed for any special social adjustment for the cost of effort (their parameter ϕ). The refinement here need not, of course, make much difference in practice.

Note also that if $f = 0$, and if leisure is ignored, this formula reduces to the standard Squire–van der Tak equation.[2]

$$\text{SWR} = w - \frac{d}{v}(w-m)$$

or
$$= m + (w-m)\left(1 - \frac{d}{v}\right). \tag{8.9}$$

If $m = 0$, then the equation (8.8) becomes

$$\text{SWR} = w\left(1 - \frac{d_a^*}{v}\right) + \frac{d_a^*}{v}f$$

$$= w - \frac{d_a^*}{v}(w-f). \tag{8.10}$$

If f is small, and if d_a^*/v is large, then the SWR can be negative. Such a case would provide eminent justifications for all sorts of food-for-work schemes.

---

2. This equation, as well as the previous one, might have to be modified in practice for nonmarginal changes. For this purpose, we can use the definition $\hat{d}_a \equiv [W(w) - W(a)]/[(w-a)W'(\bar{c})]$.

Some Limitations

All these formulations were derived from a fairly restrictive set of assumptions. For example, the industrial real wage need not be fixed. Also, if one uses differential weights—in particular those derived from the constant-elasticity valuation function—the assumption that the entire industrial surplus is reinvested might be justifiable only if the poorest persons in rural areas are not poor enough to deserve subsidies. When this is not the case, it might be more sensible to assume that a part of the surplus would be redistributed to the poor groups in the backward sector. Alternatively, one can assume that the production function, $F(L, K)$, incorporates some rural activities also, but the benefits from such activities are partially retained in the rural sector.

In such a case $\lambda = W_y(y, l_1)$, with $y = a + z$, where z is the amount transferred to the backward sector. A corresponding SWR formula can be derived from the following equation (Anand, 1981), which replaces (8.1):

$$\text{SWR} = (w - z) - \frac{1}{W'(a + z)}[W(w) - W(a + z) + (a - m) W'(a + z)]$$

$$= (w - z) - \frac{W(w) - W(a + z)}{W'(a + z)} - (a - m)$$

$$= w - (y - m) - \frac{W(w) - W(a + z)}{W'(a + z)}.$$

Equation (8.3) now becomes

$$\text{SWR} = w - (y - m) - [w - (a + z)] = m. \tag{8.11}$$

This is quite a dramatic change from the Little-Mirrlees standard formulation.

Similarly, (8.5) now becomes

$$\text{SWR} = \hat{w} - (y - m). \tag{8.12}$$

This is simply the supply price of the migrant less the additional amount available to those left behind. Of course, if the migrant were to maximize family welfare, rather than individual welfare, he would take account of the gain or loss to others. In that case his supply price would equal the SWR defined in (8.12).

In general, it is relatively straightforward to shadow price labor when labor is withdrawn from active labor markets in rural areas. Family-based peasant farming, however, presents special difficulties; no guidance can be provided on general grounds. Sen (1966, 1975) pioneered the analysis of such cases by defining a model in which the withdrawal of labor from a peasant farm leaves farm output and hours worked unchanged. Assuming a constant marginal disutility of farm labor, he demonstrated that the marginal product forgone when a *laborer* is withdrawn can be zero even when the marginal product of *labor* remains positive. While this case was relevant to the debates on the possibility of surplus labor, one can develop alternative scenarios, with or without constant marginal disutility of labor, in which farm output and labor increase or decrease when a farm member leaves.

Much depends on the utility functions assumed to characterize the behavior of farm family members, on income-sharing rules, and on the degree of concern that a family member feels for others. For example, suppose everyone on the farm consumes the average product, but each maximizes his or her own welfare, with no concern for others. Farm output is shared only by those who remain on the farm, none of it being remitted to the migrant. In this case, the remaining members on the farm will increase their hours of work after the migrant leaves if the marginal disutility of labor is constant. In fact, total farm labor and output will increase. The marginal disutility of work will be less than the marginal product of labor. This possibility, as well as others, are proven in Anand (1981).

These are some of the issues relevant to the calculation of the opportunity cost of migrant labor. The estimation of this opportunity cost requires, of course, a validated migration model, in which other markets—for example, those for land and credit—may also play a part. The initial Harris-Todaro model was inconsistent with observed rates of urban unemployment and cannot be reasonably used in practice. Nonetheless, their essential contribution was the hypothesis that migration equalizes expected wages in the two sectors, and more recent migration models use maximization of expected utility as a point of departure.[3] The basic Harberger-Harris-Todaro result that the efficiency SWR equals the modern sector wage, w, has recently been given considerable strength by Heady (1981; see also Harberger, 1976, chap. 7). However, Heady's result, like the Harberger-Harris-Todaro result, depends on the constancy of the marginal product in agriculture.

The Treatment of Leisure

In the discussion thus far, leisure has been treated just like consumption. There is a long-standing notion, however, that the leisure lost because of

---

3. Since expected utility need not necessarily be the same as the utility actually realized, the social valuation function might be based on ex post rather than on ex ante utility.

employment in a project should be disregarded in developing countries. The efficiency wage will then be zero if the output forgone is zero. The rationale for this notion has not always been made clear, but it probably stems essentially from the basic needs approach discussed in Chapter 3, with the difference that leisure is to be defined as a basic "bad" rather than as a basic "good."

Whether one sympathizes with such a view or not, its effect on the SWR can be systematically taken into account only by appropriately redefining the valuation function, $W(\cdot)$. To illustrate, suppose that the "excessive" leisure one is concerned with occurs in the backward sector only, and this lowers the utility levels of individuals in the modern sector. That is, people in the modern sector are bothered by the apparent "idleness" in the backward sector, even though they themselves take their private disutility of effort fully into account. In this case, one might formulate $U(y, l_1, \bar{L})$ as the modern sector utility function, while the one for the backward sector remains unchanged, with $\bar{L}$ being the total leisure in the backward area and l_1 being as defined for (8.5). In this case, the SWRs will be lower, since the fall in $\bar{L}$ when a person migrates to the modern sector will make others feel better off. The adjustments will, however, be additive to those indicated in the equations dealing with leisure. Alternatively, one may redefine $W(\cdot)$ as $W(y, l, \bar{L}) = U(y, l) + h(\bar{L})$ to make the penalty on leisure totally exogenous. The equation (8.6) will then be:

$$\text{SWR} = w - h' \, d\bar{L} - \frac{1}{s}(w - m) - f.$$

The SWR will decrease since $d\bar{L} < 0$, and $h' < 0$. These interpretations are only illustrative and need not appeal to those who wish to penalize leisure. They do, however, bring out the need for defining $W(\cdot)$ explicitly.

Final Remarks

In practice, project analysts need to estimate SWRs case by case, concentrating on the most important categories of labor. Such estimation will require a good understanding of the labor markets involved, so that changes in output, consumption, and leisure can be traced and adjusted in accordance with the valuation system being used.

The various formulations discussed above suggest the types of adjustment needed in practice. In some cases, exactly the same forms can be used. Conversion factors, which were assumed to equal unity in the preceding discussion, should also, of course, be introduced.

For example, suppose project demand merely displaces labor used elsewhere, with no effect on labor supply. In this case, the efficiency shadow wage rate will be m, or $m + f$ if project employment is especially arduous (the extra arduousness being reflected in f). This is exactly the same as in equation (8.7). Depending on the type of output produced by the project labor elsewhere, however, the conversion factors may differ from unity. Thus, ignoring f, and noting that m will equal the market wage rate, w, EWR $= \alpha m = \alpha w$, with α being the conversion factor for revaluing labor's marginal value product in border prices. This factor may exceed unity—as discussed in Chapter 6. In doing the analysis in terms of the foreign exchange numeraire, one must remember that the shadow wage rate in border prices may exceed—sometimes substantially—the market wage rate. If the element f is relevant, it should, however, be revalued in terms of border prices by using the consumption conversion factor, β. While in practice a general β is used, in principle this factor should be specific to the particular type of labor used.

The imposition of additional project demand may, of course, simply increase the labor supply, with no effect on other employment—as, for example, in a rural area during the off-season and without off-farm employment opportunities. If the project labor does not sacrifice previous consumption when taking project employment, its supply price will simply be βf (the value of the loss of leisure in border prices), and this also will be the efficiency wage rate. The supply price will be greater if previous consumption is sacrificed, but the efficiency wage rate will still be the same. This is because consumption transfers are assumed to cancel out in such analysis. Strictly speaking, this need not actually be the case because different persons may have different β's (this was pointed out in Chapter 6). But this is too fine a point in terms of most practical applications.

More generally, project demand may induce both additional supply and curtailment of demand elsewhere. In this case, as in Chapter 4,

$$\text{EWR} = \beta A + a\beta,$$

$A = M (E/E + N)$, E being the elasticity of supply, N the absolute value of the demand elasticity, and M the market cost of labor. Similarly, $\beta = M(N/E + N)$. Note that the placement of α and β in Chapter 4 has been reversed in this case. There might, however, be a serious problem in using this approach in the case of labor. The interpretation of the supply function for labor might be too simple, especially when the project draws labor from peasant farms (as discussed earlier).

The social pricing formulas developed above can also be helpful in practice. For example, in the off-season surplus labor situation mentioned above, and with no sacrifice in previous consumption, both the social and the efficiency shadow wage rates will equal $\beta f = \beta \hat{w}$, where $\hat{w}$ is the supply price. This follows from equation (8.10), with $w = \hat{w} = f$ (the conversion factor being introduced for this case).

The Squire–van der Tak equation given earlier (8.9)—which is the same as the Little-Mirrlees equation (8.3) except for the use of distribution weights—can also be useful for general purposes. It is applicable whenever the project wage (*w*) exceeds the output forgone (*m*), leisure can be ignored, and *w* − *m* measures the increment in consumption. If the consumption of others are affected, *w* − *m* has to be the net increment in consumption, and the same distribution weight must be applicable to others. There should be little difficulty in modifying the equation to take account of other types of assumptions. Several alternatives are presented in Squire–van der Tak.

Project work often has to proceed quickly, and perhaps for this reason a number of rules of thumb have tended to acquire wide currency. These rules—which typically imply that the shadow wage rate is substantially below the market wage rate—are often quite questionable. A few examples:

- It is often thought that with idle rural labor, the efficiency wage rate should be zero. Apart from the fact that idleness can be more apparent than real because of various household production activities, we have seen that the efficiency wage rate is not very likely to be zero. Even if output forgone is zero, the cost of additional effort need not be.
- It is also very common to estimate the fraction of rural unemployment in the area concerned, and multiply the market wage rate by this fraction to estimate the efficiency wage rate. This procedure can be justified only with very special assumptions. These are: project labor is randomly drawn from all labor subsectors, including the "unemployed," there is a common elasticity of supply from the various subsectors, and only output forgone should matter.
- It is also not uncommon to set efficiency wage rates below the market rates in very poor areas. Low productivity of labor and poverty have, however, little to do with the relation of the efficiency wage rate to the market wage rate.
- The notion still prevails that the social wage rate will typically be below the efficiency wage rate. If the social wage rate incorporates only the shadow price of investments, this cannot be true. It can be true only if full distribution weights are used, but in that case a prior definition of the critical consumption level—that is, the relative poverty line defined in terms of the valuation system being used—has to be specified in advance.
- Another common notion is that the efficiency wage rate cannot be higher than the market wage rate. As mentioned earlier, it can be, depending on the type of distortions that bear on alternative employment activities.

It is therefore unwise to suggest any mantras for either the social or the efficiency wage rates.

References

The word "processed" describes works that are reproduced from typescript by mimeograph, xerography, or similar means. Such works may not be catalogued or commonly available through libraries, or may be subject to restricted circulation.

Anand, Sudhir. 1973. "Distributional Weights in Project Analysis." Oxford: St. Catherine's College. Processed.

———· 1981. "Notes on the Theory of Shadow Wages." Oxford: St. Catherine's College. Processed.

Atkinson, Anthony. 1970. "On the Measurement of Inequality." *Journal of Economic Theory*, vol. 2 (September).

———, and Joseph Stiglitz, 1980. *Lectures on Public Economics*. New York: McGraw–Hill.

Balassa, Bela. 1977. "The Income Distribution Parameter in Project Appraisal." In *Economic Progress, Private Values, and Public Policy: Essays in Honor of William Fellner*. B. Balassa and R. Nelson, eds. Amsterdam: North–Holland.

Baum, Warren C. 1978. "The Project Cycle." *Finance & Development*, vol. 15, no. 4 (December).

Beenhakker, Henri L. 1979. *Identification and Appraisal of Rural Roads*. World Bank Staff Working Paper no. 362. Washington, D.C.

Bennathan, Esra, and A. A. Walters. 1979. *Port Pricing and Investment Policy for Developing Countries*. New York: Oxford University Press.

Bhagwati, Jagdish, and T. N. Srinivasan. 1981. "The Evaluation of Projects at World Prices under Trade Distortions: Quantitative Restrictions, Monopoly Power in Trade, and Non-Traded Goods." *International Economic Review*, vol. 22, no. 2 (June).

Blitzer, Charles, Partha Dasgupta, and Joseph Stiglitz. 1981. "Project Appraisal and Foreign Exchange Constraints." *Economic Journal*, vol. 91, no. 361 (March).

Boadway, Robin. 1974. "The Welfare Foundations of Cost-Benefit Analysis." *Economic Journal*, vol. 84, no. 336 (December).

———· 1978. "A Note on the Treatment of Foreign Exchange in Project Evaluation." *Economica*, vol. 45, no. 180 (November).

Bruce, Colin. 1976. *Social Cost-Benefit Analysis: A Guide for Country and Project Economists to the Derivation and Application of Economic and Social Accounting Prices*. World Bank Staff Working Paper no. 239. Washington, D.C.

Bruce, Colin, and Y. Kimaro. 1978. *An Economic and Social Analysis of the Chao Phya Irrigation Improvement Project II*. World Bank Staff Working Paper no. 299. Washington, D.C.

Carnemark, Curt, Jaime Biderman, and David Bovet. 1976. *The Economic Analysis of Rural Road Projects*. World Bank Staff Working Paper no. 241. Washington, D.C.

Chenery, Hollis B., Montek S. Ahluwalia, C. L. G. Bell, John H. Duloy, and Richard Jolly. 1974. *Redistribution with Growth.* London: Oxford University Press.

Cleaver, Kevin M. 1980. *Economic and Social Analysis of Projects and Price Policy: The Morocco Fourth Agricultural Credit Project.* World Bank Staff Working Paper no. 369. Washington, D.C.

Dasgupta, Partha, and G. M. Heal. 1979. *Economic Theory and Exhaustible Resources.* Cambridge, Eng.: Cambridge University Press.

Dasgupta, Partha, Stephen Marglin, and Amartya Sen. 1972. *Guidelines for Project Evaluation.* New York: UNIDO.

Deaton, Angus, and John Muellbauer. 1980. *Economics and Consumer Behavior.* Cambridge, Eng.: Cambridge University Press.

Dornbusch, Rudiger. 1980. *Open Economy Macroeconomics.* New York: Basic Books.

Duane, Paul. 1975. *A Policy Framework for Irrigation Water Charges.* World Bank Staff Working Paper no. 218. Washington, D.C.

Feldstein, Martin. 1973. "The Inadequacy of Weighted Discount Rates." In *Cost-Benefit Analysis.* Richard Layard, ed. Harmondsworth, Eng.: Penguin Books.

Findlay, Ronald. 1971. "The Foreign Exchange Gap and Growth in Developing Economies." In *Trade, Balance of Payments and Growth.* Jagdish Bhagwati and others, eds. Amsterdam: North–Holland.

Harberger, Arnold C. 1974. *Taxation and Welfare.* Boston: Little, Brown.

————. 1976. *Project Evaluation: Collected Papers.* Chicago: University of Chicago Press. Chapter 2, "Survey of Literature on Cost-Benefit Analysis for Industrial Project Evaluation"; Chapter 4, "On Measuring the Social Opportunity Cost of Public Funds"; Chapter 6, "On Estimating the Rate of Return to Capital in Colombia"; Chapter 7, "On Measuring the Social Opportunity Cost of Labor"; Chapter 10, "Cost-Benefit Analysis of Transportation Projects."

————. 1977. "On the UNIDO Guidelines for Social Project Evaluation." In *Social and Economic Dimensions of Project Evaluation.* H. Schwartz and R. Berney, eds. Washington, D.C.: Inter-American Development Bank.

————. 1978a. "On the Use of Distributional Weights in Social Cost-Benefit Analysis." *Journal of Political Economy,* vol. 86, no. 2, pt. 2 (April).

————. 1978b. "Basic Needs versus Distributional Weights in Social Cost-Benefit Analysis." Background notes for a seminar at the World Bank. University of Chicago. Processed.

————. 1982. "Economic Science and Economic Policy." University of Chicago. Processed.

Hausman, Jerry. 1981. "Exact Consumer's Surplus and Deadweight Loss." *American Economic Review,* vol. 71, no. 4 (September).

Heady, Christopher. 1981. "Shadow Wages and Induced Migration." *Oxford Economic Papers,* vol. 33. no. 1 (March).

Hirschleifer, Jack, J. C. De Haven, and J. W. Milliman. 1960. *Water Supply, Economics, Technology and Policy.* Chicago: University of Chicago Press.

Hughes, Gordon. 1976. "Low-Income Housing: A Kenyan Case Study." In *Using Shadow Prices.* Ian Little and Maurice Scott, eds. London: Heinemann Educational Books.

————·1978. "Conversion Factors and Shadow Exchange Rates." Cambridge, Eng.: Faculty of Economics. Processed.

————·1980a. "Shadow Prices for Industrial Projects in Morocco." Cambridge, Eng.: Faculty of Economics. Processed.

————·1980b. "Shadow Prices for Tunisia." Cambridge, Eng.: Faculty of Economics. Processed.

————·1983. "Shadow Prices and Economic Policy in Indonesia." Cambridge, Eng.: Faculty of Economics. Processed.

Krishna, Raj, and G. S. Raychaudhuri. 1980. *Trends in Rural Savings and Private Capital Formation in India.* World Bank Staff Working Paper no. 382. Washington, D.C.

Lal, Deepak. 1972. "The Foreign Exchange Bottleneck Revisited: A Geometric Note." *Economic Development and Cultural Change,* vol. 20, no. 4 (July).

————· 1974. *Methods of Project Analysis: A Review.* Baltimore, Md.: Johns Hopkins University Press.

————· 1980. *Prices for Planning: Towards the Reform of Indian Planning.* London: Heinemann.

Lal, Deepak, and Lyn Squire. 1980. "The Little–Mirrlees Shadow Wage Rate: A Comment on Sjaasted and Weiscarver." *Journal of Political Economy,* vol. 88, no. 6 (December).

Layard, Richard. 1980. "On the Use of Distributional Weights in Social Cost-Benefit Analysis." *Journal of Political Economy,* vol. 88, no. 5 (October).

————, ed. 1972. Cost-Benefit Analysis. Harmondsworth, Eng.: Penguin Books.

Layard, Richard, and Alan Walters. 1978. *Microeconomic Theory.* New York: McGraw–Hill.

Lind, Robert C. 1964. "The Social Rate of Discount and the Optimal Rate of Investment: Comment." *Quarterly Journal of Economics,* vol. 78, no. 2 (May).

Linn, Johannes. 1977. *Economic and Social Analysis of Projects: A Case Study of Ivory Coast.* World Bank Staff Working Paper no. 253, Washington, D.C.

Little, Ian, and James Mirrlees. 1968. *Manual of Industrial Project Analysis.* Vol. 2. Paris: OECD Development Center.

————· 1974. *Project Appraisal and Planning for Developing Countries.* New York: Basic Books.

MacArthur, John. 1978. "Appraising the Distributional Aspects of Rural Development Projects." *World Development,* vol. 6, no. 2 (February).

Marglin, Stephen A. 1962. "Objectives of Water–Resource Development: A General Statement." In A. Maas and others, *Design of Water Resources Systems.* Cambridge, Mass.: Harvard University Press.

————· 1963. "The Opportunity Costs of Public Investment." *Quarterly Journal of Economics,* vol. 77, no. 2 (May).

————· 1967. *Public Investment Criteria: Benefit-Cost Analysis for Planned Economic Growth.* Cambridge, Mass.: M.I.T. Press.

Mashayekhi, Afsaneh. 1980. *Shadow Prices for Project Appraisal in Turkey.* World Bank Staff Working Paper no. 392. Washington, D.C.

McKinnon, Ronald. 1964. "Foreign Exchange Constraints in Economic Development." _Economic Journal_, vol. 74, no. 294 (June).

Mishan, Edward J. 1975. _Cost-Benefit Analysis_. London: Allen and Unwin.

————· 1981. _Economic Efficiency and Social Welfare_. London: Allen and Unwin.

Munasinghe, Mohan, and Jeremy J. Warford. 1978. _Shadow Pricing and Power Tariff Policy_. World Bank Staff Working Paper no. 286. Washington, D.C.

Mundell, Robert. 1968. "Growth and the Balance of Payments." In _International Economics_. New York: MacMillan.

Ng, Yew–Kwang. 1979. _Welfare Economics_. London: Macmillan.

Page, John M. 1982. _Shadow Prices for Trade Strategy and Investment Planning in Egypt_. World Bank Staff Working Paper no. 521, Washington, D.C.

Powers, Terry, ed. 1981. _Estimating Accounting Prices for Project Appraisal_. Washington, D.C. Inter-American Development Bank.

Ray, Anandarup, and Herman G. van der Tak. 1979. "Approaches to Economic Analysis of Projects." _Finance & Development_, vol. 16, no. 1 (March).

Samuelson, Paul. 1950. "Evaluation of Real National Income." _Oxford Economic Papers_, vol. 2, no. 1 (January).

Scandizzo, Pasquale, and O. K. Knudsen. 1980. "The Evaluation of the Benefits of Basic Needs Policies." _American Journal of Agricultural Economics_, vol. 62, no. 1 (February).

Schohl, W. 1979. _Estimating Shadow Prices for Colombia in an Input-Output Table Framework_. World Bank Staff Working Paper no. 357, Washington, D.C.

Scott, Maurice FG. 1977. "The Test Rate of Discount and Changes in Base Level Income in the United Kingdom." _Economic Journal_, vol. 87, no. 346 (June).

Scott, Maurice FG. MacArthur J. D., and D. M. G. Newbery. 1974. _Project Appraisal in Practice: The Little/Mirrlees Method Applied in Kenya_. London: Heinemann.

Sen, Amartya K. 1963. "Distribution, Transitivity, and Little's Welfare Criterion." _Economic Journal_, vol. 73, no. 292 (December).

————· 1966. "Peasants and Dualism with or without Surplus Labor." _Journal of Political Economy_, vol. 74, no. 5 (October).

————· 1967. "Isolation, Assurance and the Social Rate of Discount." _Quarterly Journal of Economics_, vol. 81, no. 1 (February).

————· 1970. _Collective Choice and Social Welfare_. San Francisco: Holden Day.

————· 1973. _On Economic Inequality_. Oxford: Clarendon Press.

————· 1974. "Informational Bases of Alternative Welfare Approaches: Aggregation and Income Distribution." _Journal of Public Economics_, vol. 3, no. 4 (November).

————· 1975. _Employment, Technology and Development_. Geneva: International Labour Office.

————· 1976. "Real National Income." _Review of Economic Studies_, vol. 43, no. 133 (February).

————· 1979. "Personal Utilities and Public Judgments: or What's Wrong with Welfare Economics?" _Economic Journal_, vol. 89, no. 355 (September).

Sjaastad, Larry, and D. L. Weiscarver. 1977. "The Social Cost of Public Finance." *Journal of Political Economy*, vol. 85, no. 3 (June).

Smith, B., and F. Stephen. 1975. "Cost-Benefit Analysis and Compensation Criteria: A Note." *Economic Journal*, vol. 85, no. 340 (December).

Srinivasan, T. N., and J. Bhagwati. 1978. "Shadow Prices for Project Selection in the Presence of Distortions: Effective Rates of Protection and Domestic Resource Costs." *Journal of Political Economy*, vol. 86, no. 1 (February).

Stern, Nicholas. 1977a. "Welfare Weights and the Elasticity of the Marginal Valuation of Income." In *Studies in Modern Economic Analysis*. M. Artis and R. Nobay, eds. Oxford: Blackwell.

———. 1977b. "On Labor Markets in Less Developed Countries." Coventry, Eng.: Warwick University. Processed.

Squire, Lyn, and Herman G. van der Tak. 1975. *Economic Analysis of Projects.* Baltimore, Md.: Johns Hopkins University Press.

Squire, Lyn, I. M. D. Little, and Mete Durdag. 1979. *Application of Shadow Pricing to Country Economic Analysis with an Illustration from Pakistan.* World Bank Staff Working Paper no. 330. Washington, D.C.

Turvey, Ralph, and Dennis Anderson. 1977. *Electricity Economics: Essays and Case Studies.* Baltimore, Md.: Johns Hopkins University Press.

van der Tak, Herman G. 1966. *The Economic Choice between Hydroelectric and Thermal Power Developments.* Baltimore, Md.: Johns Hopkins University Press.

van der Tak, Herman G., and Anandarup Ray. 1971. *The Economic Benefits of Road Transport Projects.* Baltimore, Md.: Johns Hopkins University Press.

Walters, Alan. 1968. *The Economics of Road User Charges.* Baltimore, Md.: Johns Hopkins University Press.

Weiscarver, D. L. 1979. "Review of *Using Shadow Prices*, ed. Ian Little and Maurice Scott." *Journal of Political Economy*, vol. 87, no. 3 (June).

Willing, R. D. 1976. "Consumer's Surplus without Apology." *American Economic Review*, vol. 66, no. 4 (September).

Index

Accounting rate of interest (ARI): defined, 16; discount rate formula and, 100; discount rates and, 16; economywide estimations and, 94–95; shadow pricing of investment and, 89–90, 91; T date and, 95–96, 118; variable weight techniques and, 118, 119. *See also* Interest rates

Additive separability, social valuation and, 33, 34, 37 n.5

Aggregate welfare tests, 24–27

Anand, Sudhir, 35, 97, 137, 141, 142

Anderson, Dennis, 130

Arrow, Kenneth, 33

Atkinson, Anthony, 25 n.9, 135 n.7

Balance of payments, 15; effects of project and, 8; growth and, 44; projects without nontraded goods and, 47

Balassa, Bela, 29, 35 n.3

Basic needs, 29, 143; social valuation and, 41–43; income weights and, 43

Baum, Warren C., 6

Beenhakker, Henri L., 127

"Beneficiaries should pay" rule, 135

Beneficiary selection criteria, 128–30

Benefit levies, 134, 135

Bennathan, Esra, 130 n.3

Bhagwati, Jagdish, 46, 68

Biderman, Jaime, 127

Blitzer, Charles, 45, 46

Boadway, Robin, 25 n.7, 46

Border prices, 12 n.6, 115; conversion factor approximations and, 58; case examples of numeraire differences and, 55–58; conversion factors use and, 51, 70–73; defining SER and, 49–50; domestic cost of production and, 14; external imbalance and, 65–66; imports and exports and, 60, 61; measuring net project benefits and, 16

Border pricing rule, 46

"Border rupees," 48, 54

Border values, 13; net benefits in, 68; nontraded inputs and outputs and, 14

Borrowing, 87, 89, 100; project financing and, 84; from foreign sources, 47, 89

Bovet, David, 127

Bruce, Colin, 60 n.13, 130 n.2

Budget balance, 86, 90

Capital market issues: economywide estimation and, 92–99; formula list and, 99–101; Harberger method and, 86–88; LMST method and, 88–92; market interest rate appropriateness and, 81–83; multiple discount rates and, 79–80; shadow pricing of investment and, 83–86; social rate of return and, 77–79; traditional approach and, 10, 15

Cardinality, 33

Carnemark, Curt, 127

Cash transfers, cost recovery and, 134

"Certainty equivalent," 136

Chenery, Hollis B., 44

Compensating variations: welfare gain valuation and, 23; welfare tests and, 25

Compensation tests (Kaldorian), 25–26

Concavity, 33–34, 37

Constant-elasticity form of social valuation function, 34–39, 43, 79, 119

Consumer surpluses, 23–24, 55–58, 114–17

Consumption: distribution weights and variable weight techniques and, 119–24; distribution weights and welfare criteria and, 22–23; investment premium and, 17; shadow pricing of investment and ARI and, 90; of specific commodities by poor, 41–43; traditional approach and changes in, 10, 12–13; variable weights and changes in levels of, 109–13. *See also* Critical consumption level (CCL)

Consumption conversion factor (CCF), 60, 131; based on average consumer expenditures, 54; conversion factor aggregation and, 59; case examples of numeraire differences and, 57; shadow pricing of investment and, 106; variable weight techniques and, 114. *See also* Conversion factors

Anandarup Ray is currently the senior economist in the Projects Department of the Latin America and Caribbean Regional Office of the World Bank. He was previously the economic adviser in the Bank's Projects Advisory Staff during 1972–80.